Deceived – The Final Reckoning

By Janet Y. Perkins

BURKWOOD
Media Group

Copyright © 2018 by Janet Y. Perkins

All rights reserved. No part of this publication may be reproduced, distributed, or transmitted in any form or by any means, including photocopying, recording, or other electronic or mechanical methods, without the prior written permission of the publisher, except in the case of brief quotations embodied in critical reviews and certain other noncommercial uses permitted by copyright law. For permission requests, write to the publisher, addressed "Attention: Permissions Coordinator," at the address below.

Burkwood Media Group
P O Box 29448
Charlotte, NC 28229
www.burkwoodmedia.com

ISBN: 978-0-578-52652-2

Printed in the United States of America

Dedication

Everything in my life is dedicated to the glory of God. After that, I can only think of my husband C.W. who never fails to encourage me to "Go for it." He prays for me when I fail to ask God for guidance, holds me when I hit a wall and always finds a way to marshal his prayers through for my benefit. He is an unmatched blessing to me.

Each child has a special purpose in my life and their individual love lets me know that all the trials and struggles have been worth it – they are phenomenal people. I have plenty of associates and a few, tried and true, died in the blood friends. To all of them "Thank You" for letting me, be me, and loving me in spite of myself. Thank you for encouraging me to follow my passion to write and to let God use me.

Chapter

One

Whenever God speaks to us it's best we listen. In fact, it is utterly important to assure that you absolutely know His voice and that you purpose it in your heart to do exactly what He says. Zar was the High Priest of the Trinity Islands, and he had an especially personal relationship with God. He knew His voice and was committed to doing His will.

Mt. Mizaan was one of the three Trinity islands. He visited the mountain often. Like the name of the mountain, he was spiritually balanced. He was born to be a priest; every fiber of his being longed to worship God. He was raised in the Nazarite tradition of his ancestors. Minimally, he never cut his hair, never drank anything from grapes especially fermented wine, and never came in touch with anything that was dead or decayed.

Much like his predecessors, Samson and John the Baptist, Zar was appointed by God to be set aside as holy unto God; he was truly "Called" by God. From a young lad, he had been raised in Jubilee, which was an environment that was separated from the world and totally dedicated to the services of religion as given by The Holy One. As a youth, he was instructed that he was not to gratify the desires of his body. He was to moderate his natural affections, keep himself under control, be separated from those who trampled on the laws of God, live openly as an example of his faith in God and submit to God at all times. He was willing and reminded himself of his pledge and commitment to God daily.

Zar was powerful, not just physically, although he stood six feet four inches and exemplified a fine balance of sinews– power, vigor and resilient strength. He was at peace, in perfect balance with self and spirit. He had completely surrendered himself spiritually, and he was totally fulfilled. When he turned his head, ever so slightly, plants and bushes rustled. As he walked, tree boughs bustled with energy although there was no wind or currents of air at all. It was as though a large, unseen spirit was moving on the face of the earth. Zar was in tune with God as much as any human being could be. Yet, he fully understood he was nothing compared to the maker of heaven and earth. He knew he was dependent on Him for everything, he worshipped God in the spirit of true holiness.

He believed and lived the words of Christ who had come before him many generations prior. Of his miracles, Christ had stated that His believers would do the same miracles and more. In tune with God, Zar had experienced the fulfillment of this promise time and time again. It was his tradition to leave the mountain, once a year, and travel through northeastern Africa healing and teaching spiritual principles. He did not remain there long because the stench of willful sin was nauseating to him. He tarried just long enough to witness to others of the power of God and that He who had been faithful in the Exodus escape still lived and was worthy of total praise. As High Priest, several times a year, he also visited the School of the Prophets of Jehovah which was where he studied as a youth in preparation for his role of priesthood.

Zar was responsible for the spiritual and ethical guidance of those at the school and for the elders living in Jubilee. He took his spiritual charge very seriously and was closely in tune with the community there. However, recently he had become disturbed about Jubilee. He knew something was awry; danger was lurking close by. He felt a serious spiritual anomaly looming ominously close to his beloved Jubilee, he could feel it. His senses were alert sensing everything around him. He was ready to spring at the first inkling of trouble. He knew that he must be prepared to handle any disturbance that threatened the sanctity of Jubilee.

On this morning, he was keenly aware that God wanted to speak with him. He drew in another deep breath that expanded his lungs and chest cavity to his utter delight. The climb to the crest of the mountain would exhaust and challenge any man but, then again, Zar was much more than an ordinary man. He was chosen for this assignment. He looked around and quickly decided that it was worth the visit to the mountain. The panoramic view of the three islands, nestled together was breath-taking. He actually felt a soft gasp catch just center of his throat as he scanned the view of the islands; exhilarating and soothing all at one glance. The crest of Mount Mizaan was the spiritual pinnacle of all of them. Wedged between the other two islands, standing as an idyllic guard and reminder of why life existed and blossomed on the triune islands. Obviously, the favor of God flourished, rested and quietly settled on them.

Zar stirred and prepared to hear from God after realizing that he had been summoned to, "Come Up" to commune with Him. *"It must be something vitally important "he* mused. He was rarely invited to a one-on-one with his Maker. The first time was shortly after his dedication as High Priest of Jubilee. He spent forty days on the mountain top communing with Him. He smiled recalling the very first time that he heard that God had spoken to Moses face-to-face. As a young lad, he remembered the absolute curiosity he had wondering what it must be like to actually speak with God on a one-to-one basis. He knew the specific verses of the Torah that referenced the meeting and could recite it all from memory. Yet, each time he encountered a scripture that mentioned Moses' personal encounter with God he bristled with righteous envy and prayed one day to be able to have such an honor. He imagined what it must have been like to have stood in His presence, ingesting in as much as he could have stood of His Glory. Moses was blessed to have soaked in so much time that the spiritual DNA of God set his body aglow– the ultimate bioluminescence. How many hours had he spent imagining the Holy sensation? How many days and years had he prayed for such an encounter? He was filled with exceptional images and reminders of when God communed with other Master Guides such as Abraham, Paul and Joshua; however, none had spoken to God face-to-face like Moses had since Adam and Eve. Although he was mindful that Enoch had walked with God so much that He finally just translated him to heaven. Imagine! Talking with God personally and interacting with Him. The thought drew a warm smile and a sweet memory.

Zar awaited the dawning of another day. Finally, daylight broke the overwhelming silence of night. Darkness gave way to light; as it always must. Dawn was making her debut. Lying in the grass on the east side of the mountain, a cool, easy breeze brushed across his face. He stretched a bit, arose and bowed reverently to thank his Father for allowing him to awaken once again. The air on Mount Mizaan was so clean, fresh and pristine that he felt an immediate, revitalization. It was invigorating. He took in a deep breath, held it and let it escape effortlessly. He did this several times just to sweep the cobwebs of the evening-fore from his drowsy mind reading it for reverent meditation.

Dawn arrived in all her majestic glory lighting up the sky, ocean, and terrain of Mount Mizaan as she advanced her imminent domain over darkness. Emblazoned golden streams of light peaked from behind snowy white clouds illuminating the bluest of skies. Zar was awake. He totally loved his sabbatical visits to the top of Mount Mizaan. He was certain there was no place left on earth quite like it.

During his development as a spiritual leader, God had spoken to him in dreams and visions. He had even received personal messages in sermons and also while studying various sacred books. However, it seemed like he gleaned a significant peak into the Mind of God when standing and viewing nature. For him, nature revealed just a bit of the amazing all-consuming mastery of the Mind of God. Who, but Jehovah, could have designed such wonders in the human, animal and botanical environments? However, he recalled that he actually heard the Voice of God call him to "Come Up" to the top of the mountain shortly after his dedication as High Priest. It was there, on that special day, that he was certain never to forget that God spoke to him from a cloud that loomed, in all its majestic glory, right in front of him. Instantly, he knew to shed his shoes, for he stood on holy ground in the presence of the Great I Am. He did so quickly, bowing reverently while trying to steady himself. After doing so, he waited and shortly after, a peace consumed him, filled him like nothing he had ever experienced. Amazement circled his being, joy throbbed in his heart, his body tingled, and it was then that he noticed that his hands were aglow. He was not afraid. He was bedazzled with spiritual awe by simply being in His presence.

Zar was fully aware that "the Call of God" was the expression of God's nature in him. The Call was the threading of God's voice in him for a particular situation. Because of his personal relationship with God, he felt like his soul had been profoundly altered. Service to God was the overflow of his complete devotion to Him. He understood that God's Call was expressive of His nature and that service to God exemplified his super abounding devotion out of pure, deliberate love.

The voice of God was not at all what he expected. When God spoke to the children of Israel at Mount Sinai, the scriptures reported that "They trembled with fear and stood afar off" (Exodus 20:18). God's entrance was wrapped in thunder and lightning flashes along with the sound of the trumpet while Mount Sinai was consumed with smoke. Unlike that, his first experience with God was fascinating and compelling. His voice was strong and deliberately calm, soothing like the sound of a rippling brook. His presence totally pierced his soul, and everything in him reverently responded. He felt the Fruits of the Spirit fill him. He dwelt in a time and space he had never known before. Securely anchored to the earth and yet lifted to heights that were inexpressible, he longed to languish there forever-floating in a sea of peace and love.

God spoke to him from the cloud. Not just "a" cloud, but a cloud that was soft and billowy, strewn with cascades of colors that were white, blue, purple and silver, glassy diamond colors all melding together. It seemed to cast the light of Jasper and Sardis along with the hue of an emerald rainbow with golden flecks of light speckled within it. The cloud rested on an iridescent foundation which had a brilliant glistening aura at its core. He was totally without words to define its beauty having absolutely nothing to compare it to. No words could explain it. It was simply God adorned with a beautiful misty cloud that lovingly shielded him from certain death should he look upon God. He knew all too well that mere man could not stand in the presence of God and live. There are instances in a man's life that are unforgettable, and this was one of them.

He had traveled to the top of the mountain before. Many times, on a type of spiritual sabbatical to replenish himself and feel just a bit closer to the Father of Spirits. Sometimes the Cloud descended, and he heard his Father speak to him. Sometimes he had a heightened sense of His presence, but each visit had strengthened his resolve to totally dedicate himself in service to God. Each time he left spiritually stronger, more perfect, full and completely secure in knowing that he had a very personal relationship with Him.

The last time he had been told to "Come Up" was several years ago. God simply wanted to remind him of the history of Jubilee, the reason for the exodus from the continent and the purpose for keeping the laws the elders and priests had been given. It was a pleasant recitation of human history much like that of Moses' speech when he was preparing to die. He thought about it again and decided that his last commune with God was a "Refreshing" for he knew the laws and history well. He relished the opportunity to "Come Up" and hastened to the pinnacle of the mountain. But this time, this summons was a bit different. He felt a strange stirring in the pit of his stomach. Something was seriously disturbing; something was a foot that needed the specific attention and intervention of the Holy One. He was clear that he was going up to get his marching orders, to get clear direction on how to defeat a powerful and imminent threat to Jubilee and its inhabitants. He was ready. So, he began to prepare for the ascent to the crest of Mount Mizaan to spend time readying himself for what was ahead. He was alerted that a battle of profound proportions, a threat to the peace of Jubilee was on the precipice of time and he must be prepared to handle it. He was always ready to defend the people of God and his army, his strength was none other than the arm of God Himself. The time was now, and he would leave for the crest in the morning.

Chapter

Just northeast of the African continent, three independent islands were separated from the mainland by a strait of water just large enough for one ship to pass through at a time. Time, elements and the natural shifting of the geometric plates of earth had caused the break from the continent. The islands were uninhabited for hundreds of years standing freely just off the Northeastern part of the African coastline.

This landmass consisted of a trinity of distinct bodies of land all neatly connected by small land and water gateways. Jubilee, the largest island, Pruvia, the smaller beach, and sand-filled island and Mount Mizaan, a huge mountain stark center of an island filled with a green natural habitat that brimmed with land, sea and airborne animals of every species imaginable.

Jubilee was inhabited by the descendants of the tribes of Moses and Aaron who were of the tribe of Levites. Ephraim and Manasseh were sons of Joseph and Judah, the third born son of Jacob. Their descendants' inhabited Jerusalem during the reign of David and Solomon. Due to tribal discord and social anomalies, these tribes broke from the mainland and took up residence on the Trinity Islands. They cordoned off the land from the continent and secured a community and government founded on The Pentateuch and on the Mosaic laws given by their ancestors centuries before. The founding principles of the government were to be that the inhabitants were to be "set aside" not to dwell among non-believers as directed in the original Mosaic social rules and regulations. They established a commune based on The Commandments and Mosaic principles and lived and thrived on the triune islands successfully for over three hundred years.

Jubilee Island, the largest and primary home base for the habitation of the three islands, was so beautiful, so breathtaking that words caught in the nape of your neck when you tried to express its awesome splendor. It was not just the physical beauty of the island– not just the simple grandeur of the scenes about you; it was, much, much more.

Jubilee was not just a place, an area, an environment. Jubilee breathed life, freedom, and spirit. It was in the air, the water, plant and animal life– it was in the way the wind blew, and the ocean met the land; in a special way, the seawater kissed the shoreline. Jubilee arrested your senses and physically and emotionally possessed you when you encountered the sight of her. When you considered Jubilee in vision alone, you would automatically smile and feel lovely inside.

The island was totally alluring, bewitchingly magnificent, clean and pristine. Surrounded by the ocean, it stood as a simple beacon of truth and freedom. Each day, its ocean waves struck the pure sandy white beaches. When they did bisques of puffy, white ocean caps released a fine sea mist which moistened the air and land. Everything flourished on Jubilee. Birds of every make, kind and color advanced the land in perfect blend with animals and vegetation. Lbis, Jacana, Flamingoes, Gonolek, Sunbirds, Parrots, Pelicans, and the ever-elegant Peacock, with its elongated train of iridescent hues of blue and green all inhabited the land of Jubilee.

Janet Y. Perkins

Birds sang carols orchestrated by angels as they danced between leafy branches. Seals, tortoises, sharks, grouper, tuna, and legions of other ocean travelers romped in the crystal blue waters off the coast of this uniquely crafted island. The fauna of this island displayed all the living animals of Africa including; gazelles, barberry sheep, cows, chickens, majestic horses, elephants, zebras and more, all moving in tandem, flashing tither and yon on the mainland. Ah! Jubilee, a land brimming with spiritual charisma. The island lived up to its name–Jubilee; freeing, invigorating and calming all at the same time. Jubilee was God's vacation home.

Life was simple on Jubilee. It was very organized having governing principles that could not be compromised. Most, if not all socialization centered on the reverent worship of God. In fact, the primary reason mainland people left there to establish Jubilee was to ensure that they could follow the original biblical principles and tenets without change and adaptation. They chose to follow the unadulterated Word of God without denominational influences. Thus, the Temple was the central focus of the island, all governing rules and regulations emanated from the priests and elders who adjudicated over all matters.

One of the founding principles in Jubilee was that service to God and to His standards was not what a person did in the formal arena or as a ritualistic measure but rather how someone dealt with others. Each person must exercise his or her faith and understanding of spiritual principles by action rather than words. Every individual was the guardian, executor, and recipient of God's will and it was an individual responsibility to keep the laws of God. Social order was maintained when each person adhered to the same moral, social and spiritual mores, principles and practices. Individual and collective morality was expected throughout the community.

Although the High Priest had a responsibility to assure uniformity in the maintenance of God's law, the religious structure was founded on a belief that there was a specific and direct relationship between man and his Creator. A person had the right to go directly to God without an intermediary which was a paramount belief regarding the relationship between God and the individual. Every person was accountable to God for what he did or failed to do. The religious organizational structure adopted a standard that was predicated upon the principle that ignorance was no excuse for breaking the law. Much of the social structure focused on the Temple and reverence to God and His laws, which were continuously advanced and promoted from birth.

Akin to the judicial organizational system established by Moses via direction from his father-in-law Jethro, Jubilee had elders and judges. Zar was the High Priest on Jubilee and the representative before God. If they arose, it was the responsibility of the High Priest to bring disputes before God, to teach the people the statutes and the laws of God and to make known to them the ways of God in all matters according to the Holy Scriptures. Leaders of thousands, hundreds, fifties and tens were appointed to assist in resolving any possible disputes. Only men of good repute were chosen. Men who were honest in their financial dealings with others, moral and able to follow godly rules. Men who feared God were truthful and learned in spiritual principles were able to serve in these honored positions. These men had the ability to make good sound judgments with their morals being above reproach. These leaders were responsible for applying God's principles and were accountable to both God and the society-at-large for their administration. These men had the responsibility to execute God's law without changing one line.

The social structure was not unique in that it mirrored that of ancient times. Marriage was encouraged since it was believed that the foundation of society was the family unit. The family was considered the initiation, continuance, and strength of human civilization. The family was established when a man and a woman came together in marriage. Sexual and moral standards were high, and permissiveness was not excused but rather dealt with severely because it struck at the very core of society.

In Jubilee, young people were discouraged from seeking a partner themselves, and therefore most marriages were arranged by parents and guardians. Chastity and faith were qualities that were sought after by all parties. Since all parties on Jubilee were introduced to the same spiritual and religious principles, it was not difficult to obtain suitable partners.

The economy was formulated on the principle of honesty in all dealings. Currency and trade were conducted using denominations of Zenom's which are flat paper bills made of papyrus and other fibers indigenous to the island. The money was made by a special process which was easily transferrable into coins for trade as necessary. Work fell into several categories: farming, military, trade, education, medicine and communication/publication. Most inhabitants took pride in the farming of animals and vegetation which were traded with people by export at seaport terminals outside of the city. External markets, on the port sites, were consistently brimming with traders who sought the fresh vegetables and wholly organic, traditionally raised cows, chickens, turkeys and seafood of the island.

There was a small army of highly trained men who maintained security on the island and who were well compensated for their skill and training. Education was stressed on social and religious levels throughout the island by inhabitants of Jubilee.

Chapter

Three

She loved the quiet rain of evening and the fresh smell of the morning. She stretched a bit and felt the bed where she discovered a familiar bundle next to her. She smiled and knew that it was her younger sister Cherish. As usual, whenever the rain was torrential, Cherish found herself in bed with her big sister– snuggled up close enough so as not to be crushed should Monave rollover. *"Cherish."* She thought to herself. *"Cherish"* an actual answer to her prayers was right next to her warm and lovingly tucked beneath her.

She was so very happy with her family. She had three brothers– an older brother plus the twins. Her father and mother were excellent parents; very doting, supportive and loving but she was missing something. *"How long had it been?"* She knew the answer all too well– it had been seven years. For seven years she had prayed, every day, for God to bless her parents with another little girl and give her a little sister. Seven years. Seven years of ardently praying that God would answer her prayer and give her a baby sister to love, cherish and care for. She wanted a sister desperately but, it seemed hopeless; yet, she persisted with her prayers. She closed her eyes and reminisced for a moment.

"Mother. What do I need to do to get a baby sister?" Her mother chuckled and said, "Has Aadi been troubling you again?"

"Oh no. I don't mind him. He's just a boy. I just want a little sister. What do I have to do to get one?"

"Well let's see. Of course, you do realize that is God who decides who gets a baby and what kind of a baby it will be. Yes?"

"Yes Em, I know that, but you and Father have taught us that when we pray and believe that God will answer us."

"Yes. It is so, but that does not always mean that the answer will be yes. You'll just have to keep praying and trust whatever God says and does. Do you want me to call Jasmine and ask if Devine can spend a few days with us?"

"Yes. That would be lovely. I'm just tired of boys all around the place. And yes mother, I dearly love my brothers but…I really want a little sister."

For seven years she had prayed and then…her parents asked them to come into the dining area and sit down.

"What have you two done now?" asked Aadi. "Being the oldest I have a feeling something is up. They rarely bring us all into this area unless they have some big news. I figure you two have done something. What is it?"

Anik and Amir looked at each other and laughed. "We haven't done one thing. Angels. That's us–little angels; our mother's favorite children."

Their parents entered the room quietly. Jaya sat down and their father, Adarsh stood next to her.

"No one has done anything that we know of," said Adarsh. "We have an announcement."

Everyone looked up and waited. He continued, "Well it seems that in about six months Mo's prayer for a baby is going to be answered.

We don't know if it will be a girl, but we definitely know that we are having a baby."

"It is a girl! I knew if I just kept praying and asking that God would see how sincere I am and that He would give me a baby sister. Oh! Thank you, God, thank you, thank you, thank you!"

Mo jumped off the bench and began dancing and throwing her doll in the air and catching it. "Soon, I'll have a baby sister to hug and love and cherish for the rest of her life."

Jaya quickly chimed in, "Mo, we only know that we are having a baby. We are not sure that it is a little girl."

"It is mother; it is. I promise you it is a little girl."

Life changed dramatically in the house. The boys were all over Jaya and Adarsh could not stop asking her, "Is there anything I can do? Need anything?" They would hardly let her lift a finger until finally, she had to ask them to stop and that she was pregnant, not dying. She had to remind them she was the mother of four children and that pregnancy was not new to her.

"But you are a bit older now Jay. We were very young when we had the children."

"And now I am old and decrepit?

"Dearest, I am only concerned for you. Of course, you are not old and decrepit. You're having a baby, so obviously, you're not too old. In fact, you are more beautiful now than when we met. I just want to know if there is anything I can do for you?"

She looked at her husband lovingly and said, "Apparently, you've already done that dear." She winked at him and blew a kiss. "I'll be in the kitchen preparing dinner."

He just stood there and watched as she walked out of the room. *"I love that woman, just can't help it. Always have; I'm so very blessed."*

By the sixth month, Adarsh had insisted upon adding staff to the house to support her and to be with her when he or the children were away. He asked around and was given the name of Sharan, a local village girl. She had studied nursing and was about to sit for her certification boards. She was eager to practice her trade. School had just completed for her, so it was the perfect time for her to assist them.

The children adored Sharan. She was young and energetic, and she knew how to cook. She wasn't bossy like Maya the lady who helped their friend Taj. Monave loved her because she listened intently when she was speaking about the baby. She never discouraged her from praying for a little girl, a baby sister, but helped her to understand that it was God who made the final decision. She helped her pick out baby clothes and blankets, and she even allowed her to choose one special pink outfit that was perfect for a little girl. It was their little secret should the time arrive, and they needed it.

Time passed quickly. Jaya was absolutely beautiful. Her hair glowed, and her skin was soft and supple. She got plenty of rest, exercised daily and ate wholesome, healthy food. Adarsh came home for lunch with her every day even on days when business was booming. He didn't want to miss one minute more than necessary. She was sitting outside with friends, who were constantly around her when she excused herself to go inside for a moment. They looked at her and smiled knowing that the time was short by the way she was walking.

On the way to the restroom, she passed by her bedroom and felt the need to sit down for a moment. Momentarily, she felt a bit woozy and found that as she reached for the bed, she felt water trickle down her leg. Monave was skipping down the hall when she looked in on her mother's room and noticed her struggling to stand up.

"Mother, what's the matter? Em, are you alright?"

"Get Sharan, Mo. Get Sharan. I think my water is breaking and I need to get to the doctor."

Monave tore down the hall and found Sharan and told her of her mother's condition. Her guests left quickly so that the family could get her taken care of. Mo scurried around the house until she found Aadi and told him about the situation. He took off running to his father's business. In a total quandary as to why he was running, she picked up the phone and called her father. He affirmed that he was leaving immediately and would be home soon. She returned to her mother. Sharan informed her that she had notified the doctor but that her mother was nowhere ready to have the baby in the house. Also, everyone should relax and do as they had rehearsed. Jaya was resting on the bed with towels beneath her although the leaking had stopped.

Sharan reminded Mo where the bag was packed and that they should begin to gather her things and move expeditiously towards the hospital. Sharan called and notified the hospital that they were on their way in and also confirmed that the doctor was on the way as well and would meet them there. She heard Adarsh pull up with the car and jump out shouting orders for the boys.

"Okay. Aadi, pull the car around so that your mother can get in easily just as we discussed."

"No problem."

"Anik, get her luggage and put it in the trunk."

"Right."

"Amir, get the wheelchair out of the closet and push it next to the bed. I'll get your mother ready."

Jaya and Sharan looked at each other and chuckled. They looked ridiculous running around all scatterbrained and fickle. She sat up and got ready to move toward the car.

"No! Jaya, please just relax. We got this."

"Hmmm. Okay."

Just as planned, the wheelchair was placed next to the bed and Adarsh assisted Jaya into the chair. Out the door, they went until she reminded him that she needed her head shawl.

"Oh! I forgot about that." He grabbed a shawl off the bed and threw it around her head with one hand while pushing her toward the car with the other.

"Ad! Watch out!" shouted Jaya.

"Oops. Sorry about that. I'm good. Let's go."

Jaya stood up to get into the car when she felt arms go around her waist from the drivers' side of the car and another set pushing on the top of her head. It was Anik and Amir. One was pushing her head down, and the other was pulling her into the seat as though she was unable to maneuver herself.

"Boys. I'm okay. I can get into the car by myself."

As she was speaking Adarsh and Aadi had exchanged places, and he was preparing to drive off. Once she was settled, they headed for the hospital with the others following close behind. The hospital staff was prepared for her with a wheelchair and assisted her to her room while Adarsh checked her in.

"The patient's name sir?"

"Adarsh. That's A-d-a-r-s-h."

"How old is your wife and when did her pains begin?"

"She's forty-one, and I don't know. I'm not certain."

"And your name sir. Can we please have your name for the record?"

"I told you. My name is Adarsh. A-d-a-r-s-h. Adarsh!"

"Oh! I'm sorry sir. Then what is the patient's name?"

He stopped when he realized that he had given his name as the patient.

"I'm sorry. Please excuse me. I'm just a bit nervous. Her name is Jaya. Please send someone to the room to get anything else. I have to go to my wife."

"I understand sir. We'll take care of it."

He was off. When he got to the room, she was comfortable and in bed with everyone standing around her. Her contractions had started and stopped. He was informed that she was not ready yet but that everything was fine. She was healthy, and the baby was fine and moving into position.

"Well, what have we here? What's all the fuss?"

"Grandma! Grandma, Mother is about to have my baby sister."

Yasmin bent and squeezed Monave tightly.

"I see. How are you?"

"I'm just so eager to hold my baby sister, Savta. Is mother okay?"

"Absolutely. That's my child, and I am here to see that everything proceeds right on time as I always have."

She moved swiftly towards the bed and Jaya. She glanced at Adarsh, and the boys quickly smiled at them and then went to touch her child–Jaya.

"Eema, I'm fine. It is so good to see you."

"Did you think that your father and I would miss this auspicious occasion? The birth of our youngest grandchild is very special as they all were. You look a bit tired. Close your eyes, while I get everyone settled down. I'll be right back."

Yasmin moved swiftly to hug each of her grandchildren and to linger for an extra minute hugging Adarsh. She motioned for her husband Asher and the family to go into the adjoining room and relax. When they were there, she informed them that having a baby could be a bit challenging and that they should be quiet and prayerful until they had what everyone was waiting for–a baby. They all agreed to wait patiently and to pray for both their mother and the new baby.

It took a while–sixteen hours, but finally, they heard the soft cry of a small child and everyone looked up. Shortly thereafter, Yasmin appeared at the door with a small bundle and signaled for Adarsh to come and hold his child. He asked if Jaya was okay and was assured that she was and that she was getting freshened up and would be ready for them soon. He held out his arms and brought the baby gently to his chest. Gazing down at the small bundle he knew instantly that God had answered his oldest daughter's prayers. He turned and held the child for everyone to see. Looking at Monave, he said, "Mo, your mother and I talked about this moment and what we would do if, in fact, God had given you a baby sister. We decided to call her Cherish since you cherished the very thought of her long before this moment."

"Cherish. That's perfect. Father, can I hold her? I will be ever so careful."

"Sit next to me."

She did, and Adarsh carefully slipped Cherish into the waiting arms of her sister. He supported her back and kept his strong arms beneath her, but he allowed Monave to feel the full weight of an answered prayer.

Aadi, Anik and Amir looked at the smallest bundle of joy they had ever seen. They did not want to hold her yet and instinctively knew that this moment–this special moment–belonged to Monave. She held the baby tightly yet gently and silently prayed and thought," I *will never let anyone hurt you. I will cherish you forever and ever. Amen. I have waited for you so long, and I will forever be here for you. I love you so much Cherish. I love you. I will never doubt God again."*

There she was lying right next to her. She patted her a bit, bent and kissed her and knew that it was time to begin her day. There was never a day that passed that she did not find time to thank God for answering her special prayer; a sister–her own sister. She knew that God was not only good, but He was also understanding and knew the secret thoughts of His children. He knew that although she did not have ample words to express her total gratitude, she believed that He knew the secret, personal places in her heart.

She carefully started to rise so as not to awaken Cherish. When she moved her left foot to place it on the floor, she saw Havi's head pop up from underneath the covers. "*Havi,*" she thought. "Why did I think I could get out of here without you? Are you ready to start the day?"

Havi, short for Havilah, was a furry little black ball of soft curly fur with dark eyes. He was from a puppy litter of a dog from Havana. Her father had given him to her about eight years ago to assuage her heart when she was pining for a sister. One of the travelling merchants had him on his boat, and her father had spotted him during some business transactions. He brought Havi home, one evening in a box and sat the box down in front of her.

"I thought of you today, and when I saw this, I hoped it would be a comfort and joy to you."

"Father! What is it?"

"Open it and see for yourself."

She stopped what she was doing and bent to lift the box top. At first, she didn't see anything. She shuffled the newspaper a bit and then she saw it–something black and furry nestled in the corner of the box. She pushed aside the paper until she saw two huge black eyes open and a fuzzy black tail begin to move about. Giddy with interest, she pushed away the paper to find the most adorable little puppy she had ever seen.

"Father! Is it mine? Is he for me? Where did you get him? How old is he? He looks brand new." "Yes, he is yours, and he's about eight weeks old."

She gently picked him up and began stroking him and he responded very favorably. There was an immediate bond formed between them. She turned to her father,

"Thank you so much. He's perfect, and I love him already. I have to make a bed for him. Will you help me?"

"Of course. I have something in mind."

She set the puppy down and walked over to her father and grabbed him around his long legs. She hugged him as tightly as she could. He bent and lifted her face up, "I just wanted you to know that I never stop thinking about you when you speak, cry, laugh. It all matters to me. I thought the puppy would comfort you. It is my small way of expressing how much I love you."

For as long as she could remember Havi was her partner. When she opened her shop, she and Havi went into business. She took him with her every day and today was no different. They prepared themselves for the day and off they went.

Chapter

Batu Kadesh loved Ahshima; plain and simple he had always loved her. From the very first time that he saw her playing with her friends, he was mesmerized and she captivated his total attention. He remembered his first encounter with her clearly. There she was, about seven years old romping; jumping, twisting and turning with her little playmates. He was uncertain of the exact day and time, but his mind was filled with her laughter and giggles. Time froze when he saw the jet-black curls, slip from beneath her head shawl and press against the smooth tawny brown skin of her brow, wet with perspiration after competing so fearlessly with her friends. Batu Kadesh loved Ashima completely from that day, just about thirteen years ago, until this very moment.

Young, energetic and filled with loving compassion for everything she touched. Everyone loved Ashima and Ashima loved everyone and everything almost to a fault. She could not see an animal hungry or wounded without running to its defense. She was the mother of every child in the village and a comfort to every elderly person that breathed. She couldn't help it. She was the exact image of her mother Azaru and Azaru was like her mother Noy before her- it was genetic compassion at its max.

As time would have it, they were meant for each other, and everyone knew it. The traditional parental meeting and agreements were unnecessary, they loved each other completely. It was clear. She was his rib, and he was her covering. At every village gathering, festival, and occasion for celebration, no matter what it was, they spent their time gazing into the eyes of each other, barely breathing-just staring. They tried to be respectful, but their spiritual poles kept connecting, and they simply couldn't help it. She with those milk toasty, huge dark deer-like eyes and him with those steely deep gray-blue eyes that could pierce the armor of any foe, which when gazing at her, turned into absolute mush. The children laughed and giggled themselves into a tither about them. Mingo, the village comedian, and entertainer, always took an opportunity to "make out" over them, respectfully, cajoling about their obvious love for each other. They could have cared less if they knew about it at all. They were in a time warp-suspended animation, just floating when in each other's presence.

"Ashima, Ashima," her younger sister Deja called. "Ashima, do you want to join the dance?"

Hearing the word dance, drew her attention and Ashima turned her head ever so slightly.

"Dance? Are you preparing to dance the Mechowlah Sameach?"

"Yes! The girls are gathering now. Are you coming?"

"Of course, I'm coming silly. Don't you dare start without me."

Deja had already left having done her sisterly duty by notifying Ashima. She was off to join the others for the Happy Dance.

Mechowlah Sameach- the happy dance- was a very special dance that the women all participated in to exclaim their delight and joy with life. The happy dance was simply a celebration of life and the living of it. It was a medium for the expression of joy and the expression of other communal emotions of delight. Ashima could not think of anything more fitting for the hour. She was so in love with Batu that her heart felt the need to dance and so she broke the trance and joined the women for-Mechowlah Sameach. Off she went on the virtual wings of angels, lifted to emotional heights of love which seemed like her feet could hardly touch the ground.

When she left, Batu Kadesh felt an immediate void-the absence of air made him dizzy, and he found himself having to take a deep breath to gain his balance. He could hardly wait for her to be his wife; He was lifeless without her. *"Not long,"* he contemplated. *"Not long before she will be my wife. My beloved! My precious Ahava."* He smiled.

Momentarily, he was caught up in a dream warp thinking about her. Reveling in the moment, he realized that there were several things that amazed him. He recalled many from scriptures that were unexplained such as: how an eagle flies, how a snake slivers on a rock, how fish could live, breathe and move so effortlessly under water, how a weighty ship negotiates so well on water and how a man loves a woman (Proverbs 30:18-19). He had no explanation for any of these things- they just were. It was the same way for him with Ashima, loving her was just a part of who he was. He had heard that hundreds of years ago there was a goddess who was worshipped by an ancient tribe whose name was akin to that of Ashima's. Her name meant "Fate." Although he was clear that in no way did, he worship Ashima he loved her wholeheartedly, and he knew that God had drawn them together. They were destined to love each other. Ashima was his fate, his love for life and he liked it- a lot.

Chapter

You could not help but laugh whenever Mingo was around. He was absolutely delightful! He was born to make you smile, laugh and hurt yourself with giggles when he was near. Not the ordinary comic soul-his was a heavenly gift. God designed Mingo for laughter and creativity. Whether you were working in the fields, in the temple, in school or on the docks, Mingo could find time to turn a quip and make you laugh. He was filled with witty communications. He could talk on and on, bantering about absolutely nothing all the while tickling your innards.

While he was catching fish, he had a witticism about fishing. Something everyone had heard before but laughed just because of his delivery, his silly little antics and the way he utterly delighted himself with the joke.

"Hey, Jakeh! Why do fish swim in a school?"

"Mingo, I don't know. Why don't you tell me?"

"Silly. It's because they can't walk."

After delivering the joke, he would fall out with raucous laughter at the expression on the participant's face which was oft times a whimsical gasp at how silly he was.

"Okay I got one more," he continued. "Why didn't Noah do much fishing on the Ark?"

Deceived – The Final Reckoning

"Why, Mingo? Why didn't Noah do much fishing?"

Snickering, Mingo replied, "Cause he only had two fish. You have not been studying your scriptures Jakeh. Shame on you."

It never failed. He would fall on the ground laughing until he choked. Then, he would jump up and dance all around poking and cajoling you until you couldn't help but join in with laughter. He was amazing, and everyone appreciated his gift.

He was the youngest child of seven children born to his parents, Jael and Azu. He had four older brothers and two sisters all who lived in Jubilee. They had all grown up with his insistent jokes and pranks and had, on more than one occasion teamed up to give him a dose of his own medicine. They loved their baby brother and appreciated his desire to make others happy. However, they knew that Mingo was no fool. He was not ignorant or without any sense at all.

Rather, Mingo was very spontaneous and creative. He designed many things that were quite useful in the community. His designs and projects had afforded him quite a good living because of his creative genius so he could afford to laugh all the way to the Bank of Jubilee. He designed portable equipment for the guards that were very effective. He was continuously creating apparatus for farmers to help them to more efficiently manage their fields. Tools for educators to use in classrooms, marketing stands for use at the port for the sale of goods and on and on! His mind never stopped.

Chapter

Six

Zadok Kemet was quiet, very quiet. Slow, cool, reserved, and definite. There was no weakness in him at all. He appeared to be unemotional, but this was far from the truth, his emotions ran very deep. He hid his emotions in order that he would not become vulnerable to others.

Zadok was analytical, scientific and technical in his approach to guarding the shores of Jubilee. There had never been a challenge to Jubilee by another nation. Never been an uprising, of any sort from within. The only threat to life occurred when the children ventured a bit too close to the cliffs of the rocks. His guards often complained of the danger they faced when the children were playing unabashedly close to cliffs and clefts but other than that, nothing happened to endanger the inhabitants of Jubilee.

Despite all of this, Zadok knew better than to relax his guard. He knew the history the ancients and prophets spoke of. He knew why and how Jubilee came to be and of the escape and break from the mainland civilization. Zadok could not afford to forget. He could not relax while on duty for one instance. Keeping Jubilee and all the people and places he loved safe, was his personal mission in life.

His troops were always ready. They trained as though combat was imminent; neat, clean, fully armored and prepped to go in an instant. If any enemy approached, they would encounter an awesome force in Zadok's army. There were only 300 of them on post at any given time. 300 was more than enough to withstand any compromise to Jubilee. Each of them could run 100 yards in 9.0 seconds flat, if not better. Each man could lift 150 pounds without breaking a sweat, consistently. Each man could swim one mile in about 14 minutes and climb a steep mountain for one mile without resting. Zadok's army was extremely fit and aptly trained. They were serious about their training to handle the job. A very tight comradery existed among them, blood brothers to the bone. Their mission was to keep Jubilee free and safe from any and every menace. Their objectives were to defend the existence, territorial integrity and sovereignty of Jubilee and to deter all enemies which threatened daily life.

There was only one thing that troubled him. Only one issue, that kept alerting him, kept alarming him. One menacing thought that he could not shake and that was Devine. Devine, the daughter of Vorce, kept creeping into his thoughts. Devine, a young woman he watched grow up along with her other friends. He was older than Devine by perhaps five or six years, and he remembered her introduction to society. In Jubilee, when a young girl became thirteen, she was considered a woman and thereafter introduced as such. With careful grooming and guidance, she was prepared to be a wife and mother.

Zadok attended her "coming out" ceremony. She lived up to every scintilla of her name. She was absolutely beautiful, extraordinary as she engaged in the traditional ceremony. She was dressed from head to toe in a shimmering soft billowy white fabric, and yet her beauty escaped the covering. She was truly "divine"– a hauntingly beautiful, peaceful, loving spirit captured in the body of a thirteen-year-old girl, now a woman. A soft breeze brushed against the hem of her full skirt and exposed the teeniest, daintiest bronze ankle. Her hands were small yet strong.

He smiled when he thought of her, and he thought of her quite often. Seemingly, he found himself thinking of her quite a bit and this disturbed him. He had a lot to do, a lot to manage, a lot to take care of none of which involved a woman. A woman simply did not factor into his present equation. Nevertheless, she kept entering his space; she kept sending images of herself into his frontal lobes, and he wanted her to stop it – or did he? He sighed deeply, shook his head and decided to check on the third platoon to the north.

"No time. No time for this right now." Zadok sensed that something ominously dangerous was in the air.

Chapter Seven

After the School of the Prophets was designed and rebuilt, it stood as a beacon of historical truth, superior educational and spiritual illumination. To say that it was beautiful was an understatement, a misnomer. Jabari had received the plan in a vision, and he implemented the design as scheduled. It was rebuilt on the old site of the ancient temple. Not quite as splendid and ornate as the original temple was, nonetheless, very exquisite–it displayed an aura of simple elegance. More modern and advanced with technology than the original Temple. It was equipped with everything one needed to provide the type of lessons it was created to impart.

Large meeting halls used for gatherings and instruction were on the four corners of the edifice. In the center was an enormous cavern of space which was always used for prayer and religious services. It housed several personal lavatories and showers. Study precincts were strewn about along with a huge eating hall which provided exceptionally sumptuous meals for the students. Sleeping quarters were crafted to have two to three students per room along with their beds, a desk, lamps, sleeping gear, etc. Those who chose to attend were very comfortable. After all, they were staying at The School of The Prophets, and thus everything was incorporated for their comfort and peace. This allowed them to focus on their education which included mental, spiritual and physical instruction. The program was designed to build homeostasis in a human being, good emotional balance, and spiritual well-being.

Students from the mainland and from Jubilee attended. It was a type of coterie, a small group of people sharing like interests to the exclusion of other religious formats in an educational setting. The application process was rather simple–one merely had to assure the leaders that there was a sincere desire to learn more of the historical and biblical spiritual laws as well as those rules and regulations that governed Jubilee. Additionally, there had to be a purpose for attendance such as an ardent desire to be an evangelist, a heartfelt desire to leave the mainland and to reside permanently on Jubilee. Also, a desire to serve others in the priesthood, service in one of the professions as those on Jubilee would serve with a heart of humility and compassion. The course of study was about two years, depending on the aptitude and focus of the student. Exams were few and educational goal demonstration was vetted through one's behavior and the ability to espouse doctrine freely, willingly and on notice of a spiritual question or an open concern.

Mid-way in the twentieth century, circa 1952, Zar, and Natas met at the school and were paired up to be roommates for two years– they both were in their early twenties. Zar had been chosen, by the Elders of Jubilee, to attend the school because of the obvious "Calling" on his life. Natas had a different reason and purpose for attending the school. He had not been "Called," did not have a desire to serve his fellow man in any menial capacity and was not bent on working in any of the professions geared toward humble service. He had decided that he wanted to become a priest and to advance to a high official position as a priest and to take full advantage of all of the benefits afforded to those who lived on the beautiful island of Jubilee. Since he was not a native of Jubilee, he knew the only way to become a noted resident was to attend The School of the Prophets–and so he did.

Natas had a very interesting upbringing. Unlike Zar, he was born to parents of means who were able to allow him to partake of many of the loftier, finer things of life on the mainland. He was an only child who was spared no item of his desire. By all accounts, he was an extremely handsome child– one might say he was exceptionally handsome, far beyond the norm. Shista, his father was a very successful businessman and his mother Waiola, the wife of a successful businessman. They had servants, an expansive residence and more than sufficient finances such that they were counted among the extremely wealthy. He enjoyed the delights of his heart for most if not all of his youth. He had no particular focus, needing only to inquire about an object. He was spared the drudgery of a need for dedicated education and attention to a specific career. He knew that when his father retired, he would simply take over the business and reap the fruits of his father's labor and investments. This suited him fine since he was busy dashing about, sowing his wild oats to the delight of his father and making an absolute nuisance of himself to others.

However vain he was, Natas was an excellent sportsman. He touted a firm, lean muscular body that was focused on winning at all costs. If he did anything to perfection, it was to keep his body in excellent condition. He never failed to win first place in track and field events, he threw the Javelin precisely at every turn he took and played soccer to a fault. His father loved to attend every game of socccr in which he played knowing that his son would advance as a winner and star of the game. His father was an avid financial contributor of the game to ensure its continuance.

Soccer was an easy game to master, and Natas loved it. The most important factors of the game as explained by the originators were:

discipline, focus and the demonstration of good character and sportsmanship.

During play, if a player attempted to take the ball from an opponent, missed and made contact with the other player, this was regarded as a foul, and the fouled team was awarded a free kick. If the foul was considered too severe by the referee, the player might be given a yellow card which indicated that they were in jeopardy of being given a red card. A red card indicated that the player must leave the game and would not be able to return to play for the remainder of the game. Natas consistently received a yellow card at almost every game coming just short of receipt of the fatal red card. It was rumored among players that the referees were mindful that Shista was a major contributor to the continuance of the league and thus they were very lenient with Natas.

Natas was undisciplined in life by his parents and others in their social circle. Trouble always found him, and he fully enjoyed reveling in the excitement of deviancy. At age nineteen he joined a paramilitary organization as a means of preparing to do battle if the need should arise. Rising to the rank of a Nagad– which was a noncommissioned officer. Paramilitary forces were considered combatant forces that were military-like in intensity, firepower and organizational structure. He had no need to join. There was no imminent threat anywhere around. He just thought he might need the training in the future. He committed to two years of service after which he returned home and sought to enroll in The School of the Prophets.

As the school season opened, he and Zar became roommates and rivals competing in every area of programmatic study. At first, it was perceived as very healthy, but as time progressed, both men had to be warned that it was observed as an unholy alliance and warned that they should amend their attitudes so as to adjust and align their characters to a more peaceful mode. In order to stay in step with the schools' philosophy, they made an immediate change in their demeanors. In an attempt to assist them with neutralizing their combativeness, about three months into the school year, the ministerial staff introduced them to a new roommate–Bosher.

Bosher was not combative at all. He was a very knowledgeable, focused, peaceful and constrained individual. His goal was to live in service to others as a minister of God, as a missionary. He loved people and sought only to promulgate spiritual knowledge that would benefit others and lift them to have a more in-depth personal relationship with God. He clearly understood that "The Call" was loyalty to a ministry for God. The need to study was to show himself approved of the opportunity to follow the Calling. For him, a missionary was wedded to the charter of God. The missionary did not proclaim his own viewpoint but only that of God. Where he was placed was a matter of indifference to him, God engineered the place. He fully believed that the loyalty of a missionary was to keep his soul focused and open to the nature of God.

Bosher was fun but had no time for foolishness. He ate with them, slept with them, joined with them in all activities but did not participate in their unseemly competition. He was a perfect addition to the room, and he balanced out the energy quite well.

School activities were formulated to include social activities also. Quarterly, the school was opened to the public for them to engage in social activities with the students and staff. It was at one such event that Zar first saw Sierra, one of the young women from the village. She was about twenty-one, tall and slender with an effervescent personality that swept the room. She was delightful, energetic yet gentle with a serving humble spirit. She never failed to ask the priest's if there was anything that she could do to help them. She was always around to assist in cleaning up the area after the event in preparation for the next day and never ceased to extend her gratitude for the open invitation. She joined in all of the activities with full gusto, inquisitive about everything and fully engaged in song and music.

Zar had seen her before in the village just outside of the parameters of the school. She lived in town with her parents and two brothers Sanu and Nathaniel. Her parents were well grounded in spiritual principles and raised their children in accordance with the law. They attended the temple regularly, were humble in their demeanor and generous with their tithes and free will offerings. They, along with Sanu and Nathaniel, doted over her. She was well loved, groomed and cared for. Zar was careful with his approach knowing the rules for engagement well. He waited for the opportune time to get to know her better.

As chance would have it, at one of the quarterly open house events, she was ambling along listening to music while looking about when she tripped over a small floor plant in front of her. Seemingly, she twisted her ankle and was examining it when he spoke to her.

"Hello. My name is Zar, and I am a student here at the school. I saw your accident and wondered if I could assist you to a chair while I get someone to attend to you?"

"Oh! I was so clumsy. How silly of me. Yes. I would appreciate your assistance to a chair. And if you don't mind my brother Sanu is just over there and could help me get home. Would you mind letting him know of my condition?"

"Not at all. First, if you will take my hand so that I can attend to getting you a bit more comfortable and then I will speak with your brother."

"Thank you, sir! My name is Sierra. I am from the village, and I do appreciate your assistance."

Zar moved swiftly to extend his hand, keeping a respectable distance from her and gently guided her to a chair that was close by. When she arose from the floor, she winced when she placed her foot down such that he had to steady her with his arm. Once she was seated, he sought out Sanu. He introduced himself to Sanu and told him of the occurrence with his sister and then guided him to her side. Sanu immediately knelt to examine her foot only to discover that it was red and swollen. He removed the sash from his waist garment and carefully wrapped the bandage about her foot. Zar watched as she bit her lip and recognized that she was in pain. Immediately, he offered to garner transport to help them home. It was apparent that she could not bear any weight on the ankle. Sanu graciously accepted his assistance. Zar left and returned shortly thereafter with a means for them to get home. He found a wheelchair in the admin office which helped her to be moved comfortably and left it with them to aid her at home. He mentioned that they should not be concerned about returning it until after her ankle had mended.

"Thank you ever so much Zar. I don't know what I would have done if you had not come along."

"Yes, Zar. Thank you for all of your assistance. My family is eternally grateful for your help, and we will be in touch."

"Please don't bother yourself with that, anyone would have been eager to help her."

"Take care. I hope that your foot mends well and soon. God bless you both. Sierra, don't let this mishap detour you from coming out again."

"Surely, it will not. Thanks again."

They left quickly to get her home and off of her feet. Zar stood in the doorway to assure that they were seen off properly and then turned to re-enter the school. However, he did not go into the event but rather headed for the courtyard gardens. There he found a quiet place and sat down. He breathed deeply, sighed and settled himself. His mind was swooning, his senses swirled, and he found himself unconsciously trying to sniff the air to recapture the scent of her. *What was that scent? Lilacs? Roses? Orchid? Verbena or Blue Grass oil?* It was strangely familiar yet uniquely fresh and awakening; sweet and subtle-cleansing and cool. He was trying to sense her and trying to capture the essence of the most intriguing woman he had ever met. He prayed silently asking that God should give him the wisdom to approach this situation carefully and properly because he was certain that he wanted to see Sierra again.

About three weeks later he saw Sanu in the marketplace buying fruits and vegetables. As he approached him, Sanu turned and cheerfully greeted him recalling the situation with his sister fondly.

"Hello, my friend. So nice to meet you again, under different circumstances. I cannot thank you enough for your assistance with my sister who, by the way, is mending quite well."

"I am delighted to hear that she is well. I hope that both of you will come to the next Open House."

"You can count on it."

Sanu smiled and said, "She asked if I had seen you and if so, had you inquired about her? Now, I can respond to her affirmatively and say honestly that you have asked about her."

Zar hesitated and responded, "Of course I was curious if she was doing well. That was a nasty fall, and it was obvious that she was uncomfortable after you wrapped it."

"Yes. She was quite uncomfortable for a few days, but my mother is very astute with these things and managed to get her into a restful position relatively soon. I am certain that she will be up and about shortly."

"Thank God because it could have been worse. She was not looking where she was going. I am delighted things turned out well for her. Regards to your family! Hope to see you soon."

With this Zar, glanced down at the produce in his hands and turned to leave and pay for the objects. Just as he was leaving Sanu yelled out to him,

"I am certain my parents would love to thank you in person. Are you available for dinner tomorrow night at our home?"

He couldn't believe it! It was an opportune time to see her again. "Well, yes that would be fine with me, but it is not essential. I was delighted to help."

"Oh! My parents are eager to meet the nice gentleman who helped their only daughter, and my older brother Nathaniel, can't wait to shake your hand and thank you also. So, tomorrow night then about five o'clock?"

"Five o'clock would be perfect. I will be finished with my classes and ready for a good hearty meal and welcoming hospitality."

"That's it then. Here's our address and phone number in case something comes up. See you then."

"I'm looking forward to it. Thanks again. See you at five o'clock tomorrow."

What could happen to deter him? A world war? Nope. That would not be enough. Hurricane? Whirlwind? Major earthquake? Nope. Nope. And Nope. He was going to see Sierra again, and he very much wanted to. *"Thank you, Lord. Thank You. Thank you. Thank you."* He was gleeful and almost skipped, but that would not be the thing to do in an open marketplace, so he just checked himself and walked slowly away so as not to seemingly take off running with delight.

When he returned to the school, he sought out Bosher who had quickly become his fond, fast friend to share his utter delight with receiving an invitation for dinner at Sierra's home. He found him just where he expected, in their usual meeting place in the gardens. As he approached, Bosher looked up and saw the glow that was so obvious on Zar's face.

"What in the world have you been into? Your face is simply glowing."

"Glowing? Are you certain I'm glowing or is it sunburn?" Zar chuckled aloud having said it and immediately sat down to talk with Bosher.

"Today, my friend, I experienced the unadulterated favor of God. He totally blessed me and answered my specific prayers. Bosh, I'm having dinner with Sierra. Well not only with Sierra, but I'm dining with her family, and I'll see her again." With that Zar recited the whole day with the meeting at the market with her brother and stressed the final result being an invitation to dinner tomorrow night at five o'clock.

Bosher could scarce believe his eyes less more his ears. Was this his friend Zar? Zar, the infallible one who rarely expressed external emotions? Was this Zar- who managed to topple all records in sports and academics and stood about four inches taller than most people at the school? Bosher looked at him again, and for a moment while Zar was speaking to him, he actually thought that his friend was blushing. He closed his books and turned his full attention towards him.

"Okay. So, what's the plan? How do you intend to proceed?"

Zar looked stunned. "I don't have the foggiest idea what to do next other than going to dinner. Is there something more?"

"Hmmm. I think you should take her mother a thank you gift. Maybe some flowers or some freshly baked bread from that specialty shop over on Rosa Lane."

"Yes! That is exactly what I will do. Why didn't I think of that? Bosh, you're the best!"

"You know her father and her two brothers will be there. Should I bring something for them also?"

Bosher could hardly believe his ears. "No. Let's not go overboard. Flowers or a specialty gift for her mother are quite enough."

For a moment, they sat there gazing at each other and then, for no apparent reason they got up and hugged each other, patting each other on the back as if burping a baby. When they parted, they looked at each other and nodded signaling to each other that they individually knew that Zar was overly impressed with Sierra. No one mentioned the word love, and neither of them mentioned opening a discussion about his emotions. They just nodded and sat down.

The next day, school seemed to drag by, sports was uneventful, conversations were pleasant but unimportant as the clock slowly, ever so slowly ticked away the minutes. After the day's chores were completed, he entered the room to change and prepare for dinner. At lunchtime, he went to the market and purchased a lovely bunch of flowers and a freshly baked loaf of bread for the dinner table just like he and Bosher had discussed.

"Oh! You shouldn't have," chirped Natas, as he glared at the flowers and bread.

"Fear not my fine furry friend. These are most certainly not for you."

"Then who, may I ask is the lucky recipient. By the looks of things, they are for someone of the opposite sex. My gosh! Zar, are you actually seeing a girl?"

"Never mind who I'm seeing. Can't a guy buy some flowers without the whole world examining the timeline of his life?"

"Of course, but you, my friend are not just any guy. You must be up to something or someone. Come on and share. After all, we are roomies and all."

"Don't fret yourself about it. If there is anything significant to tell you'll be one of the first people to know."

With that, Zar turned toward the shower and dropped the conversation. Natash stood looking after him for a brief moment. He thought to himself, *"Hmm, something is up with the captain. I'll just have to investigate a bit in order to determine his plight. This is going to be good. I can feel it."*

Chapter

When five o'clock arrived, Zar found himself knocking at the door of Sierra's home. Anticipating his promptness, Sanu answered the door quickly to keep Zar from drenching himself in sweat and folding into a puddle right there on the front porch.

"Hi! You're right on time just as I expected." Sanu feigned a smile and said, "Are these for me?"

Zar flashed him a grimace and responded, "If you don't mind, I brought them and this freshly baked loaf of bread for the lady of the house and that would be your mother."

Just as he said that Marta entered the room. "This must be the handsome young man that helped my precious Sierra when she fell at the school. Welcome to our home." She graciously bowed, just slightly and motioned for him to enter the room and rest himself. Prior to doing so, he handed the bread and the flowers to Marta and said, "I hope these are to your liking." She smiled, bent and smelled them and said, "What a perfect selection. Thank you ever so much. Since the bread is so fresh, I will add it to the menu for tonight's meal."

Shortly thereafter, the sunlight in the room darkened and, in its place, stood Jehu Uriel, Sierra's father. He was a bulk of a man– not fat, just huge. He was an immense man with a warm and loving face, a gentle giant. Jehu Uriel was truly, a vast expanse of a man that filled up the whole room. Yet, although quite massive he was not intimidating in his approach towards Zar as he entered the room. He extended his hand and said, in a deep and affirming voice, "Welcome to my home Zar."

Zar could not believe the size of the man and Zar was not a little man by any means. He took in the titanic bulk of the man and extended his hand in kind. "Thank you, sir, for allowing me the privilege of dining with you and your family."

As they sat down to chat, Nathaniel, the elder son, entered the room with Sierra on his arm. She was balancing herself on the forearm of her brother as she stood to welcome Zar to her home because her foot had not yet fully recovered its strength. As she entered, Zar and Sanu stood to acknowledge her entrance. Before they sat down, Marta suggested that it might be best if everyone simply joined together at the dinner table so that Sierra would be able to settle down and not have to move again. They all responded to her beckon and retreated to the dining room.

The house was warm and welcoming; décor was that of simple elegance. It was obvious that Jehu Uriel had provided well for his family. The dining room furniture was sturdy with a delicate opulence. Zar waited for Marta to direct him to his place which she did quickly. He was seated between Sanu and Nathaniel across from Sierra who sat next to her father. To his utter delight, the bouquet of flowers that he had purchased was on the table in a beautiful crystal and gold vase. The bread he purchased had been sliced and placed on a platter for all to partake. The table was set with sumptuous delights of all types: meats, vegetables, rice and grains, potatoes, fruit, bread and two carafes of freshly brewed drinks. The table would whet the palate of anyone and Zar was hungry having not eaten for nigh two days.

Jehu stood and signaled that he was about to pray over the food. Everyone stood, but he motioned to Sierra that she could sit but she stood anyway with the assistance of Nathaniel. Jehu blessed the food, thanked the Maker and Giver of the food and blessed the hands that had prepared the food. He then reached out and shook a small bell which was a gesture for the servants to come in with the water to wash the hands of the guests. As they stood, three servants appeared with a pitcher of warm water which smelled like gardenia and a bowl. In turn, each guest rubbed the gardenia water between their hands, rinsed and then wiped their hands on a separate linen towel. After all of them had done the same, Jehu sat down, and they all followed his lead.

Dinner was served informally by simply passing the plates to and fro until everyone had what they wanted to eat. After everyone had filled their plates to their liking, Marta said, "May I call you Zar? I am aware that you are studying to be a priest and you are deserving of the respect that adjoins your station."

Zar smiled and responded, "Yes. It is my absolute mission in life to become a priest but even as such I fully enjoy being received as a welcomed visitor. Zar will be just fine." He noticed that Jehu glanced at him ever so slightly. He continued, "It will be yet another six months before I finish my studies and go before the Elders for confirmation if they deem me to be acceptable."

Sanu spoke up, "Yes, it will be another six months, but I hear that you have an excellent reputation and that based on your experience and commitment to the people you are one of those who will be considered to become the next High Priest of Jubilee."

Nathaniel joined in, "It is rumored that but for one or possibly two others you are favored to have the position you have long sought after."

Zar stopped eating, placed his fork down and said, "It is important to me that you and all others fully understand that I am not seeking a career, I am not looking for a political position and that I am fully committed to a much higher calling which is to do God's will. Being the High Priest of Jubilee is an awesome responsibility which requires faith, trust in God and a very personal relationship with Him. I take my goal and mission extremely seriously."

Silence. All eyes were upon him. He did not intend to become heavily engaged in any topic tonight, but he had to clear the air. He did not want anyone to perceive that he glibly partook of his studies or his mission.

Jehu Uriel looked at Zar squarely in the eyes, "I salute you Zar for your confidence in your calling to serve God. It is extremely important and admirable to see one so young understand the full commitment of becoming a priest, let alone a High Priest."

Sierra never looked at Zar, but he could sense that she was impressed with his response and the need for clarification of his mission. He had not fallen prey to the trap of pride that her brothers had so cleverly woven. She knew that her father admired Zar and that was unique and a very, very good thing. If there were ever going to be anything between her and Zar Jehu had to sanction it. She was happy.

The dinner concluded about an hour later, and they all walked out into the outer courtyard to rest, talk a bit and get to know each other. Zar left about seven o'clock so as not to overstay his welcome. Jehu invited him to return at any time, carefully thanked him for his help with Sierra when she fell and encouraged him to contact him should he have need of anything. Marta, Sanu, and Nathaniel thanked him for joining them and welcomed him to return again. Sierra bowed slightly, thanked him for his support when she was in dire need of assistance and left the room.

Chapter

On the way home, Zar knew that he was more than a little bit interested in Sierra. She came from a fine upstanding family which was very important to him. In due time, he would approach her father and ask if he could engage in conversation with his daughter in order to get to know her better.

Natas simply could not stand not knowing what Zar was up to. It was clear that he was interested in some girl but…which one?

"Was it that cute little pixie of a girl with the dark curls that were always escaping from her shawl? Or perchance, it was that dark, statuesque beauty known as Shasha. Hmmm, "I'll just have to get the guys engaged and find out a bit more."

He called his little minion of supporters together and told them his goal of finding out who Zar was interested in. They gleefully agreed to support his plan. It wasn't long before one of them came back with some news.

"I got it, boss. I was lurking in the garden and heard him talking with Bosher about the young woman who sprained her foot, Sierra. It seems he is quite taken with her."

"Excellent work Ganif! Excellent!"

For the next week, Natas continued to go into the marketplace until finally, he spotted her over by the pomegranates. With catlike reflexes, he edged closer to her and began examining the vegetables. Sierra was fingering the tomatoes when all of a sudden much to her surprise, they began to fall from the table. Inwardly smiling, Natas moved to catch them and help to retrieve those fallen fruits.

"Oh, my goodness!" she exclaimed.

"Not to worry miss, I'll gather those on the ground for you."

After doing so, he placed them back on the table and turned toward her. "Aren't you that young woman who was severely injured at the last social at the school?"

Hesitating for a moment, she said," I wasn't severely injured. I turned my ankle. Yes. I've been to the school several times. Thanks for your help today." With that, she turned to leave.

"Well. I'm certainly glad to find that in fact, you are okay and that the injury was not that severe. It was all over the school that you had been injured and that you were considering suing the administration to help your family with the possible medical bills."

"Sir! You could not possibly be speaking of my injury. Perhaps, someone else was injured."

"No. Did one of the students run and get you a wheelchair to help you get home?"

"Why, yes. We were given a wheelchair to assist us."

"And have you returned the chair?"

"No. Actually, it is still at my home. We were told there was no need to hurry to return it."

"Oh! Make no mistake the school is not seeking the return of the wheelchair at this time I just wanted to affirm that you are the young woman who was injured. Now, that you are up and moving about perhaps, you will reconsider suing the school for the injury. Maybe we can help you and your family in another way. Is there something specific that we can do to assist your family?"

She was furious. What an insult! To think, that her own father was incapable of caring for his family and needed total strangers to assist them in their daily living. She decided that she would not tell him. She shuttered to think of the level of his anger. Who could have spread such a vicious lie?

"I can assure you that my family never had any plans to sue the School of the Prophets. In fact, my father contributes to their mission quite significantly. How did you obtain this information?" She listened carefully to his response.

"As I mentioned, it was circulating around the school, and we were concerned if there would be a big scandal about it. I was discussing it with my roommates, Bosher and Zar, and we were just pondering the purpose of it all. After all, it was an accident."

"Zar was ever so nice to assist me when I fell, and in fact, it was Zar who gave us the wheelchair."

"No matter. You never know how these nasty little rumors get started. I don't recall him chiming in one way or the other. The important thing is that you are well."

She smiled and turned away. She didn't like him at all. There was something about him that was ominous, something sneaky and nefarious. She didn't believe his rendition of what occurred at all. Zar was upstanding and ethical. After dinner the other night, when he took the time to clarify his mission and dedication, she knew he was honest and trustworthy. She thanked him for his help and left.

After she left, he glanced at his hand and snickered for he had been successful in craftily removing the scarf she had on her shoulder. When she bent down to retrieve the fruits, it fell from her shoulder, and he quickly kicked it beneath the table so that he could retrieve it later.

She moved quickly through the market aisles so that she could get as far away from that man as possible–she didn't like him at all. What was the purpose of that conversation; that lie about Zar and suing the school? She knew that no matter the purpose it would all come to light soon enough. When she got home, she told her mother about it who listened intently and said, "Men like that are not to be trusted they are always up to some dirty little tricks which are usually for their benefit. I don't believe for one instance that Zar had anything to do with that outlandish tale. Will you check the mail for me, darling? Your father is looking for some important information."

As instructed, she began opening the mail when she discovered an invitation addressed to her. "Mother! Guess what? Cousin Azaru is announcing the engagement of her daughter Ashima, and the celebration is to be held in the large reception hall at the School of the Prophets. Of course, it is for girls only. Will you go with me? Isn't it wonderful?"

Marta smiled and said, "Of course we'll go. It will be a big affair from a very prominent family. I spoke with Azaru a few weeks ago and learned of the wedding plans. It's wonderful, and the family is so very happy with the young man she is marrying. He is Captain of the Temple Guard on Jubilee, and they have known each other from their youth."

"Em, do you think I'll ever be asked? Poppa is so intimidating that most of the young men are afraid to approach and ask to speak with me. And Nathaniel and Sanu are not much better. Ashima is two years younger than me."

Marta swiftly moved to her daughters' side and looked her squarely in the eyes, "Yes. Your true love is on the way. We must wait for the right indication from God. You don't want to be married just for the sake of saying I'm married, do you? Don't you want to experience the type of love your father and I have for each other?"

"Of course! Sometimes I think that there is no greater love than that found in the love between the two of you."

She smiled and sighed and got right back into thinking about the engagement party. She peered out the window and thought of Ashima and the fun they had as young girls visiting with each other, back and forth between her home and Jubilee. Further, she knew that Ashima totally and completely loved Batu Kadesh. They had giggled and dreamt about the two of them for years. They were meant for each other and it was time to think about something spectacular to wear to the engagement party.

Marta prayed silently for a moment. She believed that Zar was the husband for Sierra. When she met him, she felt a quickening in the pit of her stomach, and she instantly liked him. It wouldn't be long now before she, like Azaru, would be announcing the wedding of her only daughter and it was a heartwarming thought.

On schedule, the quarterly open house for the school was announced, and Sierra planned to attend. She had seen Zar a few times in the marketplace and they had greeted each other warmly. This time, she intended to watch where she was going and to definitely make certain that she was in his peripheral vision. Sanu promised to escort her and Nathaniel mentioned that he might join them. She pulled out a beautiful full flowing tie-dyed skirt with all the colors of autumn displayed. Rich rust browns, orange, fawn, and specks of gold on a taupe base sewn together in sections of six panels that were fitted at the waist and then blossomed out around her ankles. It was perfect. The colors alone were guaranteed to catch his attention.

She snapped her fingers recalling that she had the perfect scarf to go with it–one that her father had bought for her from his travels. Perfect! She began looking for it.

The day of the opening soon came, and the school was filled with people wondering about and enjoying the full splendor of the facility; she and Sanu mingled amidst them. She had never seen the Main Gardens and made a note to view them today.

"Here to see anybody special today?"

She thought to herself, *" Sanu thinks he is so cute."*

"Oh Yes! You know how much I enjoy socializing with people."

"Uh huh, but is there anyone, in particular, you are hoping to see? You know, just anyone specifically you might want to see?"

She reached up as though to pull something off of his clothing and thumped him on the side of his head.

"Ow! That hurt."

"Well stop teasing me then. You know I would like to see him, and he hasn't come back to the house again. You didn't say anything to him, did you?"

"By him, do you mean Zar? Zar, the next High Priest of Jubilee?" he said wiggling his head up and down.

"Please stop it Sanu or surely I will cry, and Nathaniel will get after you about causing it."

"Okay. Okay, I'll stop, and I promise to speak with him before we leave tonight. Perhaps, he'll come over to you if I'm here. I'll be right over there fiddling around so don't go getting into any mischief like falling and breaking your neck."

"You'll pay for that one brother when we get home."

He kissed her and was off. She waved to her friends and turned away intent on finding a path to the main garden. She took a turn and found a sign pointing to the area she was looking for– <u>Main Garden Straight Ahead</u>. It was breath-taking – full of lush green foliage and blooms of all sorts. The grass was so verdant and vibrant like a plush, velvety green carpet. Caught in a mesmerizing dreamlike state, he startled her.

"Do you want to see the most renown, beautiful flower in the garden with a smell that is undefinable?" Natas stood just in back of her. "Hope I didn't startle you, but this is one of my most favorite spots in the school." When he said that, she found that quite curious and a bit of a contradiction to his external actions.

"By the way, I have something of yours that I brought with me hoping that you would come out today." With that, he handed her the scarf that she was looking for to go with her outfit. It was her father's precious gift to her. Instantly, she reached for it and was delighted to have it back.

"I think you must have dropped it in the market the other day. Come on. I'll show you the flower before you leave."

She was overjoyed with the return of the scarf and held it to her chest as she began walking just behind him to view the notorious flower. She turned the corner after him while eyeing and inspecting her scarf to assure that it did not need repair when he reached for her tugging at her waist. In an instant, she was taken aback and shocked beyond all comprehension.

"This is the time you have been waiting for so that, even for a moment, we could be alone. No one will discover us here," he whispered.

"What! Get away from me this instant. I have no interest in you at all. I think you're disgusting and quite despicable and untrustworthy. I suggest you move quickly before I begin to call out which will bring immediate attention to your misdeeds and end your studies at the school at a minimum. Let me go!" She pulled away from him, brushed at his hand and stepped back.

"Scream? You don't want to scream. What you want is to be with me and right now we are alone." She slapped him smartly across his face and wrestled herself away intent on leaving.

"Oh! You want to put up a little fight for appearances. Okay, I got it," he reached for her again and had her in a tightening grasp about her wrists.

"What have we here?"

Natas was chagrined and very annoyed with the intrusion. "This is no business of yours Bosh. We want to be alone."

"It doesn't seem that way to me. It seems that this young lady would like to be elsewhere. Sierra, are you okay? Can I assist you?"

"Please. Please help me get to my brothers and away from this monster."

"This is none of your business Bosher. Get out of the way!"

"Guess I'm making it my business and unless you plan to interfere in my plans to escort this lovely lady to her brothers, I strongly suggest that you step aside quickly."

He looked Natash in the eyes and said, "You know you just created a storm, don't you? A big storm! I wouldn't want to be you for anything. Let's go, Sierra."

She pulled her skirts together, grabbed her scarf and fled the room in tears heading straight for Sanu and Nathaniel. Bosher waited for a moment until she cleared the room safely, turned to Natas and said, "This is bad brother, very bad. You can't leave him alone, can you? Everything he has you want and Zar is not a patient man for foolishness." He sighed heavily and walked away.

Natas smirked that devious look he had when a plan was fully in place. Bosher was right. He had no interest at all in Sierra. She was just another woman and he was focused on Zar. When he found out that Zar was emotionally intrigued with her, he knew he had found a weak spot. If he played the game just right, he could get him expelled from school and out of contention for the position of High Priest on Jubilee. Zar was in his way, and he had to deal with removing him– a bit of deception was good for the soul. Now all he had to do was wait.

Sierra fled from the hall and out of the main gates of the school without stopping to inform Sanu or Nathaniel of her total embarrassment. She simply wanted to go home and hide. Nathaniel saw what he thought was his sister running through the hall but thought that he must be mistaken. He looked around to find her or Sanu and didn't see either of them. He excused himself from his friends and decided to look for her just to assure that she was safe and sound. As he was walking about, he spied Sanu, who was having the time of his life with some fellow he had grown up with. He approached and asked,

"Have you seen Sierra? I saw someone running down the hall who resembled her a bit."

"No, but I'll go this way, and you take that direction." They left simultaneously, and before they had gotten far, they met Bosher who signaled for them to come over.

"Look, guys, you better get home immediately. Sierra had a terrible fright and left immediately to go home. She's not hurt but she is terribly troubled and probably needs her brothers right about now."

"Sierra? Sierra has been injured again?" Sanu asked.

"Nothing physical but it was quite alarming. Please go and check on her. I am certain she will be able to explain things better than I." They left immediately.

At home, she sat nestled in her mother's arms underneath her blankets with a hot cup of tea. She told Marta the whole story and how the encounter was so very disconcerting to her. Her mother comforted her and assured her that she had not done anything inappropriate or misleading. When she had left the house, she was escorted by both of her brothers which was what well raised young girls did. Further, her dress was more than acceptable; not suggestive in any way at all–she looked lovely when she left; every bit the lady. She tucked her in after she finished the tea to go give directions for dinner since she knew Jehu would be returning home soon, as would her brothers. She took a deep breath knowing that BIG trouble was just over the horizon when Jehu and her sons got together with the knowledge of this violation on their beloved Sierra. She swept out of the room with fear filling her heart not for Sierra but for the fool who had crossed the line and violated the daughter of Jehu Uriel and she dreaded the encounter. Nathaniel broke through the front door of the house out running his younger brother by mere seconds.

"Where is she?" he yelled. "Where is my sister?"

Marta stepped from a side room and stood in front of both of them since Sanu had finally caught up. "She's fine boys. She's in her room resting. Sit down. We must talk before your father gets home."

She carefully crafted the whole scene and the total deception that Natas had perpetrated on Sierra. She skipped none of the emotions that Sierra felt; none of the humiliation, none of the facts of the frightening story. Filled with rage, they listened intently to their mother knowing that she had a specific message for them. She had that fire in her eyes like she would get when one of them had plucked her last nerve, and they knew she was serious–very serious. So, they stopped and aimed their attention on her.

"I'm very concerned about many things right now. I'm concerned about Sierrra who has undergone a tremendous ordeal, but I know Sierrra, and she will recover. We will cover her with love, peace and the full knowledge that she is safe. I'm concerned because I know each of you quite well. Nathaniel, you are hot-headed just as your father once was at your age and I know how totally dedicated you are to your brother and sister. You have always felt responsible for assuring that they are safe and well cared for and you are an excellent older brother, but I do not want you to run off and handle this thing without a full agreement with the family."

"Sanu you are impetuous, fun loving, light-hearted but fully capable of allowing all of those very pure emotions to erupt and spill over into a tumultuous revolt. Please calm down until we can all talk this over together. Something is amiss here; something does not add up, but I am certain that there is something very ominous, deceptive, cunning and presumptive that is at the core of whatever is happening."

"Mother, I fully understand what you have said, however, I am the oldest, and I must do something to counteract the violent insult perpetrated upon my sister. If father were here, he would sanction this."

"You are so right my son, and that is why I'm very concerned because your father will be here shortly. He sent word to "Kill the fatted calf" by a messenger because he had been very successful in his business dealings and wanted to celebrate with his family. When he returns home, he will be overly happy and eager to share with us but will find a devastating truth about the encounter that Sierra experienced today. He will not do well with this news."

Nathaniel shuttered to think of his father in an angry state. He had seen a glimpse of it once when Sanu was a youngster in the lower grades. Somehow, one of the teachers, from a distant village, had found cause to slap Sanu and left a handprint on his face along with a lot of swelling and blisters. The man was about thirty-nine and Sanu was about seven. When Nathaniel had seen the event out on the courtyard, he ran and called his mother who in turn called his father, and the whole family converged at the school. They were all in the Headmasters' office; the teacher, the Headmaster, Marta, Sanu and Nathaniel when Jehu entered the room.

The Headmaster stood to shake his hand, and Jehu ignored him turning to the teacher he asked, "Are you the person who struck my son in the face?"

"Yes, I am, he was" …

In the flash of an eye before anyone could blink Jehu reached across the room picked the man up by his shoulders, turned him around and commenced to slap him three times in succession without missing one beat. The Headmaster opened his mouth to say something but stopped when his father looked at him with such intense emotion that his tongue seemed to stick to the roof of his mouth. When he had finished, he pushed the teacher down in a chair and said, "Get down on your knees, right now, and beg my son for forgiveness for your rude intrusion into his life. Ask him to forgive you for touching him and that you were totally out of your mind. Beg him to beseech his father not to take your life right now. Beg him! Beg him! Hurry! Quickly beg him!"

The man moved expeditiously while wincing and holding his jaw he dropped to his knees in front of Sanu who was now hiding behind Marta's skirt.

"Please, please, please forgive my foolishness for striking you. I have no idea what happened. I think I mistook you for another child. Please ask your father to release me and to forgive my foolish error."

Jehu bellowed out, "Say his name. Say, Sanu, please forgive me!"

"Sanu, dear child, puh-lease forgive me."

With that, he recalled that Jehu bent down and swept his young son up in his arms with tears streaming down his face and he said to him, "I am so sorry I was not here to protect you, son. It is only because of my love for you and my family that I will let this very foolish man live. Come. Let's go home and attend to your wounds. We'll be okay."

Standing up, his eyes blazing, he glanced around the room. Marta reached for his hand and looked at him, "Enough darling. It is enough. He is fine. Please let's go home."

He nodded and signaled to Marta and Nathaniel that they should leave. Nathaniel never forgot it. It was awesome. He had never seen the "Gentle Giant" act like that before and had never seen it since then, but the event was forever etched in his mind. Even when he punished them, he was ever so careful to pull his strikes quite a bit so as not to maim them. His father was strong, a hulk of a man and there was simply no need for him to prove elsewise. Instantly, he knew why Marta was concerned. He became pensive, calmed down and understood his mother's concern.

Sanu pitched in with understandable concern about his father recalling the dreadful day in the Headmaster's office. He and Nathaniel individually or collectively could have approached Natash and taken care of the situation sufficiently but Jehu…he shook his head. They did not have to wait long before they heard him coming down the walkway.

"Hey! Where is the fortunate family of Jehu Uriel? Where are those blessed people to be married to such a man, such an excellent negotiator and businessman? Come out, come out from wherever you are, I have really good news." He stepped onto the porch, opened the door and found them sitting in the front room with their eyes glued on him. He thought it strange since that was not his usual greeting after being away for a few days.

"Hello all," he said throwing his huge arms wide open. Marta stood to greet him. He noticed that she was not smiling.

"Where's my baby? Where is my Sierra? She would never let me come home to such a somber welcome?"

"She's lying down and will be here soon now that you are home."

Marta quickly went to hug him and then patted the couch for him to sit next to her. He responded.

"What's wrong here? This is no way to welcome me home."

And so, they began. They told him all that they knew from beginning to end. They did not spare him any details. They assured him that Sierra was fine although frightened and emotionally off center.

He deliberately asked, "Did this beast rape, my daughter?" He knew they would not lie to him.

"No! He tarnished her dignity, He entered into a sacred area of safety that all young women should expect in public, but he did not rape her. She is intact."

"Where is she? Why isn't she here to greet me? What is wrong with my daughter?"

In a low, calm yet deliberate voice, Marta responded, "She is lying down because she was extremely upset and humiliated. She was frightened also and felt helpless. She examined herself as to why he selected her to approach, and we talked about it. I am certain that she is settled on my response to her. I gave her some calming tea to settle her nerves until you came home. She wants very much to feel the strength and comfort of her father."

He rose slowly, looked around the house, glanced at his sons, nodded and walked towards her room. He knocked softly and waited.

"Come in Poppa."

Ever so slowly he entered the room he had built just for her. She eased up on her pillows and looked at her father. He moved towards her and stood near the center of the bed.

"Are you well?"

"Yes, Poppa I am fine."

"Sierra. Sierra did he …

"No! Poppa. No! I am fine he did not violate me."

He couldn't stand it. His heart– his very large heart was breaking. He carefully pulled back the blankets, unfolding them carefully and gathered her into his arms. Immediately her arms went around his neck, and she whispered,

"Poppa I'm so glad you are home."

He felt how small she was although a full-grown woman she would always be his little girl and his personal joy. He could hardly breathe. He held her close to his chest and walked out of the room with her in his arms. He entered the courtyard with her nestled close to him. He felt her warm tears easing down the back of his neck. He sat down on the corner bench where they always had their little "talks." She did not move away from him. They simply sat there.

"Sierra, in my lifetime I have been and done many things. Some of them, I am extremely proud of and some of them I wish I could change. Since meeting your mother, she has loved me in such a wholesome way that I have developed a very personal relationship with God. I cherish my relationship with Him. I fully understand the laws He gave us to live by and have taught each of my children to respect, honor and cherish them. Today will be one of the most difficult days of my life–a test-of profound proportions. Right now, if I would move, I would fail the test, for surely I would kill the man who dared to touch you with one crushing blow and the sin of it all is that I would not feel one twinge of guilt about it."

"Poppa."

"It's okay Sierra, let me finish. I love God with all my heart, but right now I cannot feel Him. I am in a spiritual quandary like I have never known. The law says that I should not kill. I agree. It says that I should be kind to my enemies, turn the other cheek, pray for those who spitefully and vengefully offend you and yet, I feel such rage within me because of my total love for you. I am going to take you back inside to be with your mother and brothers, and then I am coming back outside to talk to God and beg him to help me to quell the spirit that is raging inside of me to do that which He would not approve of."

She understood her father very well. They had many "talks" together probing into each other's hearts and souls. They were extremely close as father and daughter-kindred spirits with an extremely strong bond. She hugged him tightly, touched his arm and wiggled for him to put her down. She stood next to him and took his arm as he escorted her into the front room.

"Sierra. Dear Sierra. Sister." shouted Sanu. "Please come and sit down. Shall I get you something to eat?"

She lovingly looked at her brother, hugged and kissed him and shook her head affirmatively gesturing with her fingers to have just a little.

Nathaniel said nothing but looked at his sister and smiled. She knew him also and knew that he was struggling with an inner turmoil to do significant bodily harm to Natas. She held out her hand, he took it and came and sat next to her. Marta glanced at her daughter and knew that her inner strength would rise to the occasion and she would be a stabilizing force in this situation for the sake of the family. She would make an excellent wife and mother one day.

Jehu stood for a moment and then left the room to go into the courtyard for a bit of time with God. He opened the doors, closed the curtains and then shut them both tightly behind him. Marta knew not to approach but rather to wait for the test to end. For now, she would marshal her family together so that they could enter into corporate prayer for their father and her husband to meet this tremendous spiritual challenge. They would intercede, fast and pray for a man they all wholesomely loved and cherished. They would pray that their family would be able to withstand the test with him.

Chapter

Ten

Zar finished his orals with the priests and ran to change clothes for the last game of the season against a rival team from another city. They were in the championship finals which meant that to win would bring notoriety to the school and a large bonus check that would extend many ministry programs. He had been chosen to be captain of the finalist team, and he was really excited. He hesitated for a moment and went over his responses to questions posed by the Committee to make recommendations for the priesthood and ultimately for the High Priest position on Jubilee. He was not worried. He fully believed that if God wanted him to have the position, it would be so. Truthfully, he really wanted to return home as the final candidate for the position but was settled to be in the will of God. He dashed up the steps to get ready for the game.

The shower felt really good, warm, relaxing and yet it invigorated him. He knew the players on the other team and their strategy and felt confident that by pulling together, his team would emerge victoriously. Stepping out of the shower he dried off and began to dress in the team uniform when Bosher entered the room.

"Hey! You better begin to get dressed for the game. I know we have some time but…"

Bosher looked at him and said, "Sit down. We must talk before the game. We have plenty of time." Zar snapped the towel at him and gleefully said, "Not feeling butterflies, are we?"

"Butterflies? I'm feeling a lot of things, but butterflies are not counted among them."

He sat across from Zar and carefully constructed the whole story, brick by brick, watching every expression on Zar's face. He stopped and waited.

"I have no choice."

"Yes! You do. God always gives you a choice."

"This is one violation that is specifically aimed at me, and I will be all too happy to oblige his challenge."

"My dear brother, we have become fond, fast friends in the time we have spent together sharing intimate secrets with each other. I'm no Zar, but I can assure you that I can hold my own in any challenging situation."

Zar nodded in total agreement. He knew who Bosher was and he knew what damage he was capable of.

"It was all I could do to keep from engaging in a full-fledged battle right there in the gardens. I have held so much in for so long with his arrogance, selfishness and continued propensity to twist things to his satisfaction in order to totally deceive his victim. I wanted to injure him in the worst possible way, and the only thing that stopped me was that I was just returning from some intimate one-on-one time with God in preparation for my orals tomorrow and the game tonight. I had a wonderful, peaceful encounter with God and was filled with the warmth of His all abiding love when I stumbled onto Natas and his nefarious scheme. Perhaps, it was no accident. What do you think?"

He continued while Zar listened.

"Yes! I was ready to spring and devour him like a hungry lion on a weak little rabbit, but I did not. Why you may ask? Simply because I had been with Him. His Spirit filled me so that it quelled the spirit of Satan that would have loved to have the fight which would certainly have expelled me from school, the game tonight and surely out of any consideration for a position as a priest which is what I came here to do."

Zar's muscles were dancing, his arms and back were tight, his eyes were glazed over with a film that made them look like black hot coals and fire danced in them. He asked, "How bad was it? Was she crying? Did he damage her clothes?"

"I explained this to you already. Before he could actually do any significant physical damage, I was there, and I stayed there until I knew that she had left the grounds safely. It was very strange though Z because he didn't look so disappointed about her. He even had a strange glint in his eyes like an animal that is just about to capture his game. I took note of that look and asked the Holy Spirit to reveal its meaning to me. Listen to me! You know I would not feign such a report–this is the revelation I received."

Zar turned towards him and paid full attention.

"It was not about Sierra. She was only a ploy. She was the enticement, the apple, the bait. It is really all about you. Think about it. If he could engage you in a fight and spin a tale, as only he can do, to make it look like you attacked him for no reason, then you would be knocked out of the running for a position as a priest and most definitely out of consideration for the High Priest assignment. You would have to forfeit your position as captain tonight, and you would highlight the embarrassment of someone you care a lot about. Knowing him he would most certainly have them questioned why she was in that area of the garden, she was not raped; her clothes were not damaged, soiled or disheveled by him positioning it all as a figment of her imagination to get attention. What a mess! He is the great deceiver and not worthy of being considered for Priesthood. Natas is the citadel of obstinacy and evil. God in you is stronger than the spirit he serves."

Zar sighed heavily and pondered the wisdom of his friend. He was not at peace, but the truth had to prevail. Natas was a cunning foe and had craftily chosen a soft spot for him which was Sierra. Somehow Natas had determined his genuine concern and care about Sierra. Then, he used her as the ploy to cause him to fall. It was the same old game but different garden.

"Okay. You're totally right. I have an affirmation in my spirit. However, you need to know this is not over."

"Oh! I know it. Vengeance is mine sayeth the Lord, but sometimes He leaves a little room for us to taste a bit of it also." They shook hands and hugged each other. "Let's get ready for the game."

"I'm good. Get dressed. I'll be right back."

Bosher looked at him intently.

"I'm okay, really good. I fully accept what you said to me, and I am in full agreement. I'll be right back."

Zar swiftly left the room, turned right at the corner, moved stealthily down the hall, hitched another right and waited. He prayed for strength, timing, and patience. It didn't take long.

"Ow! What?" yelped Natas.

"Oops!"

Natas had entered the corridor fully intent on returning to his room to engage Zar and get dressed for the game. He was delighted to see that his ominous plan was in full effect and would shortly be fully implemented. He turned left and ran full force into the right elbow of Zar. The strike was so forceful, so dynamic that he stumbled back trying to gain his footing and ran right into Zar's left leg which caused him to fall forward and back again striking a hard marble table straight on knocking him out cold. Zar sprang into action and called out to acquire help for him since he was totally unconscious.

Several people responded to the call for assistance and got him to a medical facility. He was unconscious for several hours due to a significant concussion, failed to show up for the game or his orals and was laid up for several days. Zar's team won the finals, and he was named most valuable player. He and Bosher tag teamed the best they ever had anticipating each other's every move. As the game concluded he said to Bosher, "Game over."

"I knew it. God slid you a little piece of vengeance, just enough to keep you in the game and in His will. God always wins. Always."

Chapter

Monave couldn't help herself. Anytime he was near her she knew it, her body sensed it. His pheromone scent was picked up immediately when he was in the area. Who could blame her? Jezreel was six feet six inches tall, bronze, built and bold. He exuded strength and he was powerful through and through.

He had a quiet demeanor, but there was no question that Jezreel owned the space that he occupied at any given time and place. He was captain of the troops who guarded the internal perimeter and ports; an extremely important, respectful and essential position. She never looked directly at him, never made deliberate eye contact. She knew her place, she knew the rules. Essentially, in Jubilee, "A man findeth." So, she remained busy knowing that when he was near if she stopped, he would sense her interest, her desire, her longing to be his wife. She already belonged to him. He just didn't know it.

Years ago, Jezreel's forefather, Jabari walked more than 1,173 miles gathering support, from every person and community he came across to rebuild the old Temple site for the School of the Prophets just as the Spirit of God had directed him to. Jezreel was determined to continue in the tradition of his forefathers. He had more than earned his esteemed position as Captain of the Guard. He had responsibility for overseeing the total area of the inner city which included the Temple and the safety and security of the citizens in Jubilee. His men were well trained, as trained as those who guarded the exterior area of Jubilee. History had taught them that a tribe, a community, a legion, a principle government of any sort might just decide to try to overcome Jubilee; this was totally unacceptable. He loved Jubilee. He loved his life and the choices he had made to commit to serving God in spirit and in truth. He had determined to do whatever it would take to maintain their lifestyle.

She knew that he was on tour with his troops inspecting everything in the city since the trade was about to begin on the port. She and Havi went about preparing her goods for customers by opening packages, setting up candles and soaps so that they could be smelled and seen quickly. She had designed some new scarves, belts, and skirts that matched perfectly. They were certain to be a big hit. She was very excited about promoting the new line of jewelry she had developed and began placing them on shelves for display when she heard someone enter the shop. When the door chimes rang, Havi came out to greet the new customers and stopped.

They entered the shop and began looking around. There were two of them–traders or ship helpers apparently looking for something special. She noticed that Havi did not move but continued to stare at them which was very unusual.

They seemed a bit scruffy which was normal for sailors and tradespeople.

"Good morning. Can I help you find something?"

"Good morning. We're just looking around. If we find something, we want we'll let you know."

"Fine, I'll be right over here."

It wasn't long before a few other customers entered the shop and engaged her in conversation. Her business was very popular on the pier because of her unique clothing designs, specialty soaps, oils, and jewelry. Monave was very creative with an excellent reputation, and her new jewelry line was getting quite a bit of attention. She was busy attending to several ladies who had questions and one tradesman that was extremely interested in her jewelry. The two sailors who had entered earlier left after glancing around. Once they left, Havi was back to his usual playful, social behavior.

She had a phenomenal day with sales. She made an excellent and very beneficial contract to provide a ship owner with jewelry exclusively for external sales not associated with Jubilee. She was exhausted and was about to close the shop down for the day when the two sailors returned.

"Oh! Have you returned to purchase something?"

"Yes. We want to purchase two of these necklaces and two bracelets to match them."

"Oh my! Unfortunately, I cannot sell them since I have committed them to one of the ship owners and I was just preparing them for packaging to conclude the sale."

"But we saw them first, and we made up our mind that they were just what we needed. We have the money, and we would like to take them with us now."

"I'm so sorry. I wish I could sell them to you, but I've given him exclusive rights for sale outside of Jubilee."

"Well, if he wanted them, he should have taken them with him when he was here. Here's the money for these two necklaces and bracelets."

He placed the money on the table.

"Sir, I do appreciate your desire for the jewelry, but I cannot sell them, and I'm preparing to close the shop for the day."

"Well, we seem to have a problem since we plan to leave with the items."

Havi circled the store and began to growl soft and low. It was apparent that he did not like the visitors who were in the store.

"I really don't like dogs, so it's best you move him away from me and begin to place those items in a bag for me. If you can't seem to get them together, we can do it for ourselves."

With that, they moved to pick up the items and take them.

Monave knew these two sailors were going to be difficult, so she pushed the buzzer that Mingo had rigged up for her under the table to alert security.

"Perhaps I could interest you in these scented soaps which are lovely gifts. Or, I have just added these beautiful scarves and skirts to my line. They are just out, and no one has them yet."

"Jewelry– We want the jewelry we saw earlier today and nothing else. Now get them ready right now. Please don't make me have to retrieve them myself."

With that, the sailor and his friend moved toward the shelf and grabbed the items they wanted. When he did that, Havi jumped up and ran toward one of them barking and making a huge ruckus. The bigger one picked up his foot to kick at him when something stopped him.

"Gentlemen, are we being polite and keeping the rules that have clearly been given to everyone if you want to conduct business in Jubilee?"

Jezreel stood directly in front of them both with his feet squarely planted on the floor.

"You weren't thinking of kicking that dog, were you?"

They knew him, and they knew not to cross the captain. They stepped back a bit and looked directly at him.

"We're here to purchase some items, and once we have them, we'll leave."

Jezreel glanced at Monave.

"I explained to them that the items were not for sale since I have made an exclusive contract with one of the ship owners, but they won't accept my explanation."

"So then, that concludes the matter. The items are not for sale, and the shop is about to close."

He looked at them both and pointed to the door. They turned to leave the store.

"We'll leave now, but we'll be back, and those items better be here."

Jezreel moved in back of them so quickly that it startled everyone. "Is that a threat? I hope that was not a threat. Tell me was that a threat?"

Before they could answer, he pushed them out the door and stood quite near to them.

"You two are not welcomed here anymore 'cause I don't like your attitudes. Give me your passes right now and return to your ship. Do not. I repeat "Do not" step onto the pier again at any time. Do I make myself clear?"

They shook their heads, gave him their passes and headed for the ship. When they were totally out of sight, he turned to go back into the shop.

"Are you okay?" he asked Monave. "I'm so sorry you had to encounter that. I will make certain to have a guard stationed closer to the shop in the future since your business is so prominent and busy." He smiled and looked at her trying to determine if she was still frightened.

"Oh, I'm fine. It was a bit nerve racking especially when I thought he was going to kick my little Havi. You came just in the nick of time. Thank you."

"That buzzer Mingo had placed in here was a great idea. I think I'll encourage other merchants to have it installed. Just so happened that I was very near when I saw the light flashing."

"I never thought I'd have to use it. I've never had any sort of trouble in the store. Thanks again."

"Well, I'll wait for you to close the store and walk you down the pier so that I can know that you are safe. You won't have to worry about those two ever again."

"Okay. I'll close up and get my things together. It'll be just a minute. Havi come on we're closing."

She had never been so close to him before, and she hoped she wouldn't faint dead out. His voice was much deeper and stronger than she had imagined. She popped something sweet and minty into her mouth to freshen it and grabbed her bag. *"Providence. It had to be providential for him to have rescued me."* She managed to get her keys, turn out the lights and exit the store without tripping all over herself while trying to keep her composure.

He stood near her, looking down to make certain the door was locked and then waited for her to walk in front of him a bit while he escorted her from the pier. Once she was inside of Jubilee proper, he bid her farewell and said he'd be checking on her. She floated home and into her mother's kitchen.

"Em. You'll never know what happened today." And she proceeded to tell her the whole story. Her mother listened carefully, smiling while she was overseeing the meal preparations. Instantly, she knew that her daughter was smitten, and she didn't blame her. She knew exactly who Jezreel was and the excellent reputation he maintained. *"We'll see,"* she thought, *"we'll see."* Jezreel would be perfect for her eldest daughter.

Chapter

Twelve

Jehu entered the garden and went into solemn and reverent prayer. He had to speak with God because if he didn't, he knew he would violate every spiritual principle that he believed in. Natas' violation of Sierra totally shattered him emotionally and spiritually. There was wrestling going on within him that was shaking him to his very core. The battle between the Master of Light and the Master of Darkness raged within him. He was struggling to serve God as he totally believed. He had submitted his will to God and chosen to serve Him totally. Yet, Satan was staging an awesome battle in his mind by using his emotions and his love for his daughter. Satan was using all the weapons in his arsenal–deception was primary. Deception, the art of making someone believe something that is not true. He knew Satan was staging a battle for his soul; he knew the tricks he was playing with his mind and emotions. He had a history with Satan–tests that he had failed on his way to finding truth, peace and a personal relationship with God. He did not want to revisit those old emotions, those old tricks that soothe your emotions and make you lose your footing with God.

He was struggling because all of him wanted to do significant bodily harm to Natas. If the truth be known, he felt rage at the level that he could easily have squeezed the very life from him without a second thought and he knew it was wrong. He was weak and needed to seek God. He tried to think of scriptures and righteous thoughts that could help ground him in this instance.

"Give me a clean heart and renew a right spirit within me."

"Father, please breathe on me."

"Blessed is the man that endureth temptation; for when he is tried, he shall receive the crown of life, which God hath promised to them that love Him."

"Be swift to hear, slow to speak and slow to wrath for the wrath of man does not produce the righteousness of God."

"The fruit of the Spirit is love, joy, peace, longsuffering, gentleness, goodness, faith, kindness, and self-control."

Self-control? Love? He knew the scriptures and the meaning of them, and most importantly he knew that love was the most important one. Why didn't his heart stop racing? Why was his pulse racing through his veins as though he were facing an extreme adversary? The answer was simple. He was facing an adversary, a foe much stronger than him, one who was skilled in the art of deception. The only way out was to ask God to help him to overcome the battle that raged within him.

The evening drew near, and Jehu was weary. So, he decided to lie down and rest. He would rest there in the garden and pray that an angel would visit him and touch his heart so that he could let go of the consuming desire to take the life of Natas.

The next morning, he found warm water and a clean towel with which to freshen himself. Next to it, he found a bowl of fruit, warm bread, and soothing tea. "*Marta,*" he whispered her name. "*Marta,*" she had loved him with a deep, thorough understanding love and he did not want to disappoint her trust in him. It was Marta who had led him into a deeper relationship with God. She exemplified all the goodness that ever existed in mankind in his mind. She had been patient with him when they spoke and was able to quell the spirit in him that was wild, outspoken and brash. She tamed the beast in him that would strike out in an instant when he was affronted by anyone. He knew no fear of a person. It was not merely because of his size. It was because there was a spirit within him, a "Peter-like Spirit" that would strike out without realizing the consequences of his actions. "*Marta.*" The thought of her calmed the savage beast within him and he turned to pray and talk with God.

It took him three days to quell the urge to kill, strike, maim. Three days of beseeching God to help him. Three days of wrestling with self so that he could rise victorious and still feel the satisfaction of vengeance having given it to God. He smiled and rested on the words he knew were of God, "Do not take revenge, leave room for God's wrath, for it is written: It is mine to avenge; I will repay." He searched the scriptures and found solace in the words of Paul. Paul knew what he was going through and expressed it well in the seventh chapter of the book of Romans.

"I do not understand what I do. For what I want to do I do not, but what I hate I do. And if I do what I do not want to do, I agree that the law is good. As it is, it is no longer I myself who do it, but it is sin living in me...I have the desire to do what is good, but I cannot carry it out. For I do not do the good I want to do, but the evil I do not want to do–this I keep on doing. Now if I do what I do not want to do, it is no longer I who do it, but it is sin living in me that does it. So I find this law at work: Although I want to do good, evil is right there with me. For in my inner being I delight in God's law; but I see another law at work in me, waging war against the law of my mind and making me a prisoner of the law of sin at work within

me…I myself in my mind am a slave to God's law, but in my sinful nature a slave to the law of sin."

It was settled. Is there any revenge that is more thorough than that taken by God? He thought not. His relationship with God was deeper and more profound than ever and he had grown stronger spiritual muscles. He had passed the test of fury, a wild feeling fed by the beguiling emotions of Satan which were designed to inflame his wrath to kill Natas and forfeit his standing with God. He had learned many lessons about himself and more specifically about what God expected of him. He recalled the words of the prophet Micah, *"What does God require of thee? It is to do justly, love mercy and to walk humbly before Him."*

He finished his test review of self, by thinking of the words of David. David a man after God's own heart; David who had sinned and repented and written such beautiful words of love to God as those mirrored in the twenty seventh Psalm, "The thing I want I seek most of all, is the privilege of meditating in His Temple, living in His presence every day of my life, delighting in His incomparable perfections and Glory." He was prepared to stand down and to let God be God; assuredly God did not need his help. He opened the doors to his home and entered into peace, love and rest.

Chapter

The Happy Dance–Mechowlah Sameach. Oh! How she loved it. All the women gathered together, young and old, and celebrated life and the living of it; they celebrated the goodness of God in dance. She ran directly into the gathering of women as they lined up to prepare for the celebration. She heard the music and the metered beat of the drums. Her heart sang for she knew why, among other things, she was dancing. She was going to marry Batu–soon, very soon. Joy, inexpressible joy, filled her heart, mind, and soul. She was so very grateful that God had allowed him to choose her from among so many other beautiful women that would have been all a flutter to marry him. *"Batu"*–she felt her feet begin to pat, her toes eager to wiggle and stretch themselves as a part of the dance expression.

"Ladies, please gather over in the far corner so that we can begin the celebration."

It was so endearing to watch the older women stand and move to join in the preparation. She totally loved her elders. They were so graceful and poised filled with wisdom that they were eager to share with the younger women from the village. They knew stuff. Stuff about cooking, healing, how to manage their families, children and husbands, how to balance careers with family duty. They had helped her numerous times, and by listening to them and her mother, she had the blessing of being chosen as the wife of Batu Kadesh.

The music summoned them, and they made a circle by initially holding hands and moving slowly around in the circle until someone felt a need to openly express their utter joy. Usually, the younger women stood back and gave the floor to those who were older. It was Azaru, Ashima's mother, who began with her joyful expression. She moved out gracefully from the circle with her hands lifted high. She was overcome with happiness at the soon approaching marriage of her daughter. Her first expression was Barak which was a bow in true reverence to God. Joy has always characterized Israel's corporate worship life, and she knew the Happy Dance well from childhood. It was an appropriate expression to initiate praise. Surprisingly, Noy, Ashima's grandmother, joined her daughter in praise and worship with a smooth, light shuffle that indicated her delight and joy in the God of all heaven and earth. This was quite unexpected since Noy was so advanced in age although her back was still straight and her legs still strong. It had been many years since Noy had actively danced with the women although she had joined the circle many times. Once, many years ago, Noy had been the dance leader eager to offer praises to God. Now, she offered a quiet spiritual poetry of gratitude in dance for His many blessings.

It did not take long for the younger women to join in with praise and worship at a much higher dance pitch. Several of them offered the Guwl which is a move that allowed the dancer to move around in large circles with great joyful emotion. Dance was perceived as a soothing yet reverent way to express delight in praising God. It was not a technique but rather a means of declaration that came close to expressing the inner language of the heart. As the spiritual life matured so did the way, you expressed your love in reverence to God and like fine wine, the dancer matured with every performance based on her personal spiritual relationship with God.

Ashima could not wait any longer; her heart was bursting with joy, and she broke from the circle with the praise of Hallal. Hallal praise in dance is the expression of intense love and adoration for God. Its purpose is to manifest God in the midst of praise, to enthrone and honor Him in dance. She incorporated many Alat jumps of joy in her performance. Her purpose was to praise, celebrate, glorify, rave and boast of her love and reverence for God. She was thankful with such joy that she could only dance her feelings out and that was the whole point of the Mechowlah Semeach– the happy dance. She danced with such delightful expression that she mesmerized those who watched.

"This is what the Angels must feel when they rejoice and bask in the glory of God."

She swirled on and on in an open full out declaration for gratitude until she knew that He understood her joy.

Chapter

Preparation had started for the fulfillment of his highest dreams in life. Zar was chosen to be the High Priest on Jubilee. He had overcome many challenges, especially the test with Natas. He stood still, closed his eyes and silently thanked God repeatedly. He smiled inwardly realizing that Bosher would also be joining his team of priests. He and Bosher had been through so much together. They had become best friends and brothers. *"Jubilee,"* he took in a long deep breath and finished preparing for the installation ceremony.

Bosher looked in the mirror quizzically and wondered, *"I know God never makes a mistake, but I can hardly believe that I will be among the priests in Jubilee. It is more than a dream come true. I prayed so much that I thought it was too much for God."* He smiled and quickly turned to finish dressing so that he could join Zar for the installation celebration.

Family and friends gathered in the sanctuary of The School of the Prophets. Reverent music filled the hallowed halls of the school as guests filled the room in anticipation of the reverent services. The Deans of the School took their places and initiated the ceremony with a welcome to the guests and an explanation of what was to take place. Shortly after, the candidates entered the room and waited for the ordination to begin. One by one, the priests who were finalists had their names called and were given recognition of their honored new stations.

Finally, Zar was called to take his place as the ordination service progressed and he was named as the High Priest of Jubilee. He was given a written document signifying his station and the responsibilities he had with respect to assuring the teaching of the Torah. As a final act of the ordination the current High Priest who was retiring approached him and reaching up placed his hands upon his head to signify the change in leadership on Jubilee. Because he knew Zar since a child who had grown up under his leadership, he took a special moment to kiss both sides of his face and to bless him.

In the fashion of David, Zar turned and knelt before the altar and prayed aloud for God to bless his leadership and to guide his every move on behalf of His people who lived in Jubilee. He stood and faced the crowd bowing before them. He raised his hands with the palms facing forward and the thumbs of his outstretched hands touching. The four fingers of each hand split into two sets of two fingers each forming the letter Shin (symbolizing that God has not changed); simultaneously he chanted the Aaronic blessing over them.

"The Lord bless and keep you, the Lord make His face to shine upon you and be gracious to you, the Lord lift up His countenance upon you and give you peace."

It was done–Zar was now responsible for the spiritual, physical and moral growth and development of the Trinity Islands.

Chapter

Azaru had a wedding to plan – Ashima and Batu were getting married and the time was quickly pressing in on her. She knew the colors that Ashima wanted, and she knew who Ashima wanted to stand beside her- it was Monave her cousin no doubt about it. Batu chose his best friend, since childhood, Jezreel. Jezreel was the perfect man to honor the ceremony and stand beside his friend as a witness before all heaven and earth.

So much to do; so much to plan for–food, music, wedding attire, accommodations for those coming from outside of Jubilee, floral settings, the Chupah, the Ketuba review... her mind was racing. Joseph simply watched his wife skirting about running to and fro like a little ant hoarding food for the winter months. He smiled realizing that weddings were for girls. He knew Batu was the perfect man for his daughter–he worried no further. Yes. It was important that everything went smoothly. Yes. It was important that there was enough food and accommodations. Yes. They all had to look nice. He realized that it was all important to "them." His only concern was that Batu was a man of God, that he was more than able to care for his daughter, that he was well respected and that he would meld into the family well. He gave Azaru open access to whatever funds she needed to make the wedding memorable to the women he loved so dearly. He asked his wife if there was anything that she needed him to do knowing full well that she would say, "No. I'm fine." He smiled at her fidgeting with patches of fabric strewn across the table and left the room leaving her to her wedding plans.

Deceived – The Final Reckoning

For days Ashima, Azaru, and Noy fretted over the smallest details. Finally, they sent for Monave to come down to calm her cousin down and to spend some one-on-one girl time together. It was perfect timing for Monave who needed to get away from the shop for a few days after that harrowing experience with the sailors. Of course, Jezreel had taken total charge over the whole situation, and she had never seen them again, but still, it would be good to see her cousin and join in the planning.

By the time Monave reached Jubilee Ashima, and Batu had already met with a priest, received counseling and selected a date for the wedding. The wedding invitations had been selected, and she fully agreed that they were exceptional. It seemed like all of Jubilee was invited to share in "The Joy of the Wedding." The house was all a twitter with plans and activities associated with the wedding until finally, the day had arrived. The biggest decision was about the Chuppah. They decided that the Chuppah, which was a canopy that the couple stood under symbolizing the home that they would make together would be in a circular pattern indicating their unbroken bond together. It was splendid- strewn with beautiful white flowers, gold cord and laden with flowing shimmering white fabric.

Fundamentally, the ceremony followed that of the Torah with few changes. The Ketuba had been given to Ashima and her father. Batu gave the wedding dowry to her father which was accepted gracefully. Ashima agreed to the wedding contract and drank the cup of wine that Batu had poured for her signaling that they had a blood contract. After Ashima drank the wine that Batu poured for her, he gave her a special gift and left. Once committed to each other and prior to the wedding day every time that Ashima left the house, she would cover with a veil indicating that she was engaged and had been "bought with a price." Monave knew that the veiling custom followed the biblical story of Jacob who had worked for seven years to marry his beloved Rachel only to have been tricked by his father-in-law. Unbeknownst to him Leah, the older sister, had been substituted for his beloved Rachel, under heavy veils at the wedding. There was no danger of that happening for this wedding, but it was a tradition that had meaning. The wedding really began after Ashima had been veiled.

The families were situated properly just outside of the Chuppah- the groom's family on the left and the bride's on the right. The priest entered the aisle taking his place at full center followed by Jezreel who stood to the left of the Chuppah. Batu followed and stood under the Chuppah to the left of Jezreel. Monave slowly entered the aisle standing just to the right of Batu under the Chuppah.

Ashima covered in a lovely soft white veil came next escorted by her parents stopping just before the Chuppah. Her parents then stepped to the right side. After her parents were in place, Ashima then took three steps which symbolized her decision to enter the marriage and Batu came to escort her under the Chuppah. The priest read the Ketuba aloud, and the couple sealed the ceremony by drinking the wine together; conjoined bliss.

Chapter Sixteen

"I didn't get a chance to tell you about our good fortune from my business trip. Now, that things have settled down a bit let's discuss it." Jehu looked at Marta with an anxious smile beaming across the expanse of his whole face. It was clear that he had some really good news to share with her. Not only was his news good but he thought it would break the tension in the house after the whole debacle with Natas.

She stopped what she was doing, sat down, folded her hands and turned to her husband. "Come on, tell me about it before you bust or that smile totally overtakes your whole face, and I won't be able to recognize you." He chuckled at her wit.

"Well, not that I'm smart or anything. Not that I'm a really good businessman and negotiator but…I've made the deal of a lifetime. I have a twenty-year contract not only to design the ships for the contractor but to oversee building them."

Marta raised her eyebrows and then lowered them. She lifted her head and quizzically looked at him.

"That's right! Our business has just tripled over the next twenty years plus. As smart as I think I am, I must give ALL honor to God for his unmerited favor. Marta, our income has tripled, and I have a significant check in my pocket to seal the deal. God has simply poured out a blessing that is immeasurable for us. I scarce can believe it!"

Quickly and deliberately she rose from her seat and went to her husband. She looked him squarely in the eyes, reached up, captured his face in her hands and kissed him. Then, with all of her might, she hugged him and whispered, "Not for the money, not for the luxury that will come but for your obedience to God and to loving us so much. Thank you for all of your hard work and dedication to us. The only words I have to give you is to say how very much I love, respect and willfully submit to your governance over this house. You have done well darling, and God is rewarding you; rewarding you with His favor."

This massive man, this huge, bulky expanse of a man became like a small child. "All a man wants from his family; his wife and children is to earn their love and respect. Everything I do is for you. The fact that you appreciate it makes it so very sweet and endearing. Thank you for loving me. Thank you for keeping this home going when I've been away. Thank you for being my very best friend for all of these years." They embraced, and then, simultaneously they went into the courtyard and praised and thanked God for the overwhelming blessing that He had bestowed upon them.

When they arose from prayer, she poured a soothing cup of black seed tea for him as they sat across the table from each other.

"Marta, I've been thinking."

"Um hmm."

"I won't have to travel so much now. In fact, I've got to set up a site for manufacturing and design rather quickly. I wonder would you consider moving the family to Jubilee and leaving the mainland. I've got a plan in mind, but I will not proceed until I know your thoughts and feelings about moving to Jubilee." She sipped her tea, put it down and said, "Husband where you go, I will follow."

They laughed out loud each knowing that she could be very fixed at particular times. "Well, it might be the best thing to do at this time. I can see the immediate benefit to you for design and manufacturing. The business would surely flourish there. Plus…it seems that Zar and Sierra are quite serious about each other and he is now the High Priest there. If their relationship should mature, as I expect that it will, we'll already be living there. We have the boys to consider, but with good, clear corporate planning for the family it could work."

He clasped his hands entwining his fingers together and began to tell her his plan. He would speak to Nathaniel about managing the business on the mainland until they could move everything to Jubilee. It would mean that he could stay at the house during the transition an also oversee the sale of the property. He would be needed in both places as things progressed, but it would be a wonderful opportunity for him to become more involved with the business. Of course, Sierra would move with them, and Sanu would assist with the design plans as he always had done. In fact, he would be closer to Mingo, his creative buddy, and together creativity would surely abound for the business. She thought his plans were prudent and that he had carefully considered many vital things. They decided to speak to the family.

Marta planned a special meal and asked everyone to attend. Right on time, they entered the dining room. Nathaniel, looked elegant, as he always did. Tall like his father yet slimmer in the shoulder and waist. He was dressed in a white linen Neru-type jacket with crisp black linen slacks and sandals. Sanu dressed in a printed free flowing dashiki which was adorned with an elegant lace trim and coffee colored slacks. He was such a creative and gregarious spirit.

You could tell he loved and welcomed people by the way he dressed. Sierra sauntered into the room in her lady-like fashion appearing alive, vibrant and engaging which is why her father and brothers adored her. She was well and looked hauntingly beautiful at dinner. They took their places for dinner as each remarked at how lovely the dinner table was dressed.

Jehu blessed the food and then, told them about the contract to design and sell the ships and the financial favor of God. He laid out his plans for the future of the business and moving to Jubilee. He completed the whole business scheme and move and then concluded with,

"Your mother and I have discussed this, and we agree to it. However, we are a family, and we want your input."

Nathaniel spoke first, "Hmmm, now let me see if I heard you correctly. I'll oversee the management of the business here and ultimately incorporate the move of it to Jubilee as well as oversee the sale of our property here. Is that correct?"

"Yes. It is," affirmed his father.

"And I'll move to Jubilee and handle design. As I have all along but on a larger scale. Plus, I will be able to entice Mingo to work with me. Is that right?" said Sanu.

"Yes, Sanu you are correct."

The brothers, who were sitting beside each other glanced at each other, stood to their feet, raised their hands and saluted their father.

"Yes! We're in."

They then winked at each other and sat down. Smiling at them, Jehu shook his head, nodded and returned the salute. Sierra was quiet for a moment and then spoke up saying,

"I think this is a good thing. Sometimes change can be very beneficial. It'll take some adjusting, but I cannot imagine being away from my family. I like it. Let's do it."

They all agreed to the plan, and then the three children of Juhu Uriel took their goblets of freshly squeezed pomegranate and grape juice, stood and saluted the man at the head of the table–husband and father to them all.

Chapter Seventeen

Shortly after the ordination service, Zar and Bosher moved to Jubilee. Once there, the elders greeted them, gave them a quick tour of the temple facilities, introduced them to staff and left them to discuss their new responsibilities and surroundings. Rather than sit at his office desk, Zar sat next to Bosher on the couch as they had done so many times at school.

"Well brother, our dreams have come true. We have the opportunity to serve God in ways we never imagined while simultaneously blessing the people of God."

"I take this whole assignment very seriously Zar. I've lived for this moment, and I hope you know you have my full support. I am more than a priest who reports to you. I genuinely love you–you are my brother." After speaking, Bosher looked at Zar, and they nodded.

"Bosh, Jubilee is growing. People want to come here because of the way we live and worship. With growth comes a challenge. I'm thinking of regionalizing Jubilee. I'd like for you to consider developing a community and religious center on the west side of the island. There are already people moving and congregating there, and I want to assure that we keep a good handle on things. We can meet with Jezreel, who is the temple captain here and Batu Kadesh is his second in command. Zadok guards the whole perimeter of the Trinity Islands." Bosher nodded his head in approval.

Deceived – The Final Reckoning

The next day Zar met with the elders of Jubilee and expressed his plan of action and concern about the growth of Jubilee. They met for several hours, had the plan committed to paper and began to put it into action. It was agreed that Batu would specifically guard the inner perimeter of the religious center on the west end of the island and report to Jezreel. In order to maintain a cohesive worship standard, the Temple would continue to be the main sanctuary on Sabbath with ancillary services at the west end center. There was a lot of work to be done, so they began immediately.

Zar installed Bosher as the Priest in charge of the west end development project and placed three elders under him to support religious and community development. Builders were requested to meet with the elders to draft plans for the new west end center. A general contractor was selected, and a date was set to begin construction. In addition to building the west end center, housing plans were drafted, roads and utility supplies were etched out which included plans to disturb as little of the island habitat as possible.

As priest and second in command to Zar, Bosher had responsibilities at the School of the Prophets as well as missionary work. He spoke to Zar about making a mission trip as soon as possible so that he would be available once the west end development construction began. Zar agreed and assigned him to an impoverished community in the western part of Africa where there was an established missionary refugee retreat and small hospital that was supported by Jubilee. Once he had his home near the Temple established, he left for Africa and the missionary retreat known as The Canaan Center.

The Canaan Center housed one hundred twenty-three initially destitute children with food, clothing, medical care, and an educational facility. Canaan school stressed worship– inclusive of the rules of the Torah and Mosaic principles, health and wellness, character development, sports, the arts, etc. Conjointly, Canaan incorporated youth counseling for the children due to the abusive conditions from which most were rescued. Once found and rescued, many children were determined to be severely malnourished, sexually abused, whipped, scarred and burned oft times over their entire bodies. This required more than prayer, it mandated medical and mental treatment and a loving, supportive touch. Canaan was just the place for them. Jubilee priests were always on hand to assist as were educators, medical technicians, counselors and a plethora of volunteers. The Council of Elders on Jubilee were especially pleased with this missionary assignment and continued to send funds to support staff to maintain it and see it grow. Both Zadok and Jezreel sent a contingency of soldiers to maintain a safe and homeostatic environment for all.

The western end of Africa was well known for having marauding local tribes as well as slave traders from other countries enter its villages and take adult men and women to sell. Further, they sought small children as personal and sexual slaves for themselves and affiliates. Human trafficking was a lucrative business which marauders pursued feverishly without any effective restraint.

About eight weeks after his installation as a priest Bosher left on his mission trip to The Canaan Center. As a student at the School of the Prophets, he had been to Canaan several times. Each time was a stark reality of the sin dredged world that existed. Each time he left more committed to serving God and mankind than before and each time his heart was mauled with grief at the sight of the condition in which he found the children. He found horrific circumstances that he tried to push from his mind but failed to do so. Children so badly abused that his eyes actually flowed with tears that he could not voluntarily cease. Children so poorly treated that you could not imagine that it was at the hands of human beings, not rabid animals that caused their condition.

He had to steady himself for what he knew he would encounter when he entered Canaan. Although their lives were bleak when they were brought to Canaan, God had blessed the facility to care for them in exemplary ways. Loving, caring, soft and warm hands touched them– sometimes for the first time. Nourishing food was prepared for those who could handle eating solid food. A milky drink of herbs and vitamins was prepared for those who were unable to chew and swallow whole food.

Facing these severely negative conditions filled with the carnage of evil men spilling their hateful ways onto small, innocent children never deterred Bosher from ministry. He never questioned God– never blamed God but rather committed to worship Him for putting up with such a sin-filled world and yet He continued to love us. He put the blame for the world's condition exactly where it belonged– onto mankind and the choices made since the beginning of time. He was clear. He served a loving God filled with compassion, mercy, and love for a world gone astray from His original plan. It was settled for Bosher. He determined that the purpose of being a missionary, for him, was so that he could be God's servant; one in whom God would be glorified. He often wondered how God continued to love us. *"Why is God so patient with us?"* The abomination of all manner of abhorrent sinful ways was a stench in the nostrils of the maker of the universe and yet–He lingered and suffered long with us.

When he thought of Jubilee and the beauty that abounded there, he was able to get a mere glimpse into the majestic and beautiful mind of God. Thinking of the awesome wonder of the complexities of the human body assured him of how intricately we were made. He was certain that God would not take so much time creating the world and all the numerous types of life that flourished under, on and above the earth only to destroy it all. No! He was certain that God was love and determined that he had no concept of what we as a people, would do if God took His Hands from us. *"Where would we go? To whom would we appeal for help?"* And so, he pressed on in service to God and mankind.

He got right to work once arriving at the Canaan Center. He checked in, introduced himself and took inventory of the specific current needs. He was informed that both Zadok and Jezreel were in-house and had plans to make a raid on a marauder's camp that had recently captured and stolen away twelve village children from a nearby tribe. Immediately, he set out to locate his new friends. He found them strategizing with a platoon of forty men for the evening's strike on the camp. They welcomed him in by standing at attention and once signaled to relax advised him of the strike strategy.

It was dangerous! Marauders are unscrupulous people, without conscience or decent characters who were motivated by greed and selfish concerns. Bosher did not hesitate to authorize the plan and advise that he was going along. Both Jezreel and Zadok knew that Bosher was physically and spiritually ready to lead and participate in the strike. If the plan was executed perfectly, they would be able to recapture the children and whisk them away without the loss of life to either side. Their goal was to advance upon the camp in the wee small hours of the morning, sweep into the camp, awaken the children and carry them away while the marauders slept. However, should an adversary approach any one of them in an attempt to thwart the rescue they would reap the full wrath of God's forces in a mighty way without any hesitancy.

Bosher left to suit up, prepare himself spiritually and mentally. He prayed for God to bless the attack and if possible, to disable the adversaries without spilling blood or taking life. But, if either blood or life had to be sacrificed, he sought God's favor for his troops. Time quickly advanced, and the team of forty assembled and moved out.

As expected, the camp was quiet with only a campfire burning and three guards sleepily on station. They were overtaken swiftly from behind and put to sleep with the apt administration of a unique type of sleeper hold–they were out cold. Quickly, the troops pressed toward the tent where the children were housed. Some soldiers stood guard on the exterior of the camp.

Other soldiers were stationed at key points inside of the camp while others approached the children, retrieved them and exited the campsite. Not a peep was made by the little ones. They all slept right through it, nestled safely in the arms of God's Forces from Jubilee.

On notice, one by one the soldiers in the inner camp stations moved out and joined the exterior forces. When it was determined that all were accounted for, in unison, they moved away from the campsite. As the children awoke, sometime later, they found that they were at the Canaan Center. As their sleepy little eyes opened, they looked about to find a clean facility, the smell of good and warm and loving faces welcoming them. Amazingly, none of the children seemed startled by the new environment. None of them were crying. However, they looked about curiously. Very carefully, the staff moved towards them. From the midst of the crowd, the head counselor, Libi advanced and began speaking to them slowly and softly. She told them who she was, where they were and why they were there. She advised them that the only concern was for their well-being and that a bath, clean clothes, and food awaited them.

The children did not make one sound but willingly followed the beckoning invitation of Libi. All twelve of them took warm baths, were given fresh, clean clothes and were taken to a place to eat. Not one child spoke and no one uttered a word. However, their eyes were dashing about, taking in everything around them.

While the children were being cared for Jezreel and Zadok met with the troops. They prayed together and thanked God for His favor in the maneuver. After prayer, they debriefed and examined what they could do better or differently. They discussed counter strategies and amendments for more effective and efficient strikes on other camps. They determined that they knew of seven other similar camps within the area. Plans were set into effect to rescue the children in those camps. Reconnaissance troops were sent out to each camp to obtain as much information on the layout of each camp and return with the intelligence data. Within the next two weeks, they had raided six of the camps successfully and brought all of the children to the Canaan Center without a challenge.

Seeing the condition of the children was difficult, and yet it inspired the troops to keep pushing themselves. Bosher stepped away from the militia and went into the center to check on the children most recently rescued. It was there that he met Libi. She was quite striking in a unique type of way; not so much a physical beauty but her spirit and inner beauty filled the room. Clearly, she was extremely sensitive, caring and compassionate while touching and speaking with each child. She knew all of their names and had adeptly compiled data on each of them. She knew what tribes they were from if their parents were alive when they were taken, how much education they had, their health condition, spiritual beliefs and the traumas they had endured. She had a masterful dexterity when caring for children. Bosher was quite impressed with her passion for the children. He approached, "Hello. I am the senior elder and priest from…"

"Jubilee. I know. Thank you ever so much for caring and attending to our needs."

"No need to thank me. I am charged with the responsibility of missions and evangelism and more specifically for overseeing and reporting on the Canaan Center. You are doing an exceptional job. We should thank you."

Libi smiled, "Thank you. There is so very much to do here. I hope what happens here makes a dent and matters."

"Most assuredly it does not only to the children but most importantly to God. Service to others always gets His attention."

"Oops! It's noon. Gotta' go and tend to my little flock. Nice meeting you. Don't be a stranger."

With that, she whisked away leaving an obvious tremendous void of energy in the room. Bosher smiled knowing that the children in the Canaan Center were in good hands. He left to get some much-needed rest. He was off of his normal schedule by not eating or sleeping properly for the last several weeks.

The recon team for the seventh kidnapping campsite had returned. They rendered their debriefing report to their respective leaders, and it was obvious some things would have to change. This troop of marauders were significantly larger, heavily armed with artillery and had three tents filled with children of all ages. They set out to hatch a plan. For five days the recon team took note of all activities in the camp. They watched all of the older children and noted where they were located in the camp. When an older male child went to relieve himself in the woods, Jezreel approached him and quickly advised of the rescue mission. The child paid strict attention to him. He was ten years old and through the grapevine had heard of rescue attempts before. He understood what they wanted and readily agreed to assist as long as he had a promise that his sister, who was in another tent, would be rescued. Jezreel gave his word. Seth, at ten years old, agreed to marshal the children together and advise of the rescue attempt so that they would not be startled and give the rescue mission away.

Secretly, Jezreel met Seth for three days and explained that the rescue would be the next day early in the morning. Seth told him where the guns were kept and how the camp was structured. He also told Jezreel not to forget about his sister. For ten years he was pretty savvy; he had been through and seen a lot for those ten years. The plan was set. Earlier the night of the strike two soldiers stole into the artillery tent and emptied the guns of all ammunition and then returned them to the prior position. They searched the tent, which was unmanned at that hour, for all artillery and disabled or disposed of it all expeditiously. Anyone peering into the tent would not suspect a thing. Then, careful fine slits were perforated at the rear of the tents filled with the children so that they would pull apart quickly for escape. Next, four foxes that had been captured were to be turned loose in the camp as though they were hunting for food. They had been deprived of food for several days and just given water, but no meat and they were crazed for sustenance. Swiftly, soldiers stationed fresh meat near the tents of marauders around and about the camp. Finally, a cage of poisonous snakes were to be released about the same time the foxes ran through the camp creating quite a good diversion.

When the plan was executed, a shock wave of excitement and distraction ran through the camp. The foxes were ravenous and would not be deterred from the fresh meat they sensed. Snakes wriggled everywhere frightened and trying to escape detection and certain death. Marauding soldiers ran screaming and yelling trying to avoid the venomous snakes and rabid foxes while Jubilee soldiers stealthily opened the tents and began guiding the children away.

The two captains did not expect to get away so easily but only positioned themselves for a minor diversion just long enough to retrieve the children who were ready and waiting due to Seth's prior advance warning. A few feet away from the tents, Jubilee soldiers were waiting to defend the children as soon as the marauders determined that they were gone.

It didn't take long before the molesters ran to the tent to retrieve their guns and pursue the children. There were only about thirty of them who took after those who had dared to attempt a rescue mission in their camp. All of their hard work was escaping into the woods. They could not allow it and regrouped to pursue them in rapid fashion.

Seth searched the faces of the children for his sister and did not find her. "Hey! I do not see my sister. Kila is not here. Go back for her as you promised."

Jezreel looked down at the young lad and nodded. He signaled for the troops to go on without him as he planned to keep his word and go back for the young girl. Bosher overheard him and decided to override his order and go for the young girl himself. He decided that Jezreel would be needed more to assist his troops with the battle that would ensue if the marauders caught up with them. Bosher turned to Seth, "If your sister Kila is in that camp and she is alive I will return with her. Go and help the others escape." Having spoken, he turned toward the camp and left.

He stood in the wings of darkness dressed in the foliage of the woods as the marauders passed by in hot pursuit of their prey. He waited for a moment for any stragglers and then headed for the camp. He was exhausted, but he prayed, *"God give me strength and the wherewithal to save that little girl."*

He pressed on until he reached the camp in short order. He stood quite still and listened intently. He heard a slight whimper coming from the first tent on the left. A shallow light was beaming forth illuminating the shadow of a portly man about five feet ten inches tall. He eased quietly toward the tent.

"Shh, now my dear! I will not hurt you. I've had my eye on you all along desiring you for myself. The bounty I would receive for you will be heightened if I break you and teach you how to please a man. Plus, I am enamored of you for you are exceptionally beautiful for one so young. Come now, let me show you the delights of being with a man."

Kila whimpered and tried to unloose herself from the shackles that bound her. He tried to kiss her, and she withdrew her neck in retreat.

"Don't make this so hard dear. Submit quietly, and I promise to be easy with you."

"Please sir," Kila begged, "I have done you no harm. I do not know you. Please let me go so that I might find my brother and return home."

Samir laughed out loud. "Do you think me a fool? You will fetch hundreds of dollars at the auction if I do not keep you myself for trade. You are not going anywhere."

Samir loosened his shirt and released the snap on his pants. "Come here my pretty."

"Will I do? I might not be pretty, but I'm more than willing to tangle with you."

With that Bosher lunged forward with a forceful thrust and yanked down Samir's pants, pulled his shirt twisting him about, struck him in his groin and proceeded to knock him out with one quick blow. Samir folded onto the floor. Without wasting a minute, Bosher unleashed Kila, pulled her clothes about her and helped her to her feet. She was just a child–albeit quite a striking young girl. Quickly, they scurried from the tent and headed for the forest when they heard it.

"Click, click"- the sound of an active gun.

"Now was that nice? I have done you no harm sir, and yet, you come into my tent, steal my goods, my bounty, strike and maim me and then attempt to run off unabashedly. Thus, I think this is not a good motion. Do you agree?"

Bosher pushed Kila behind him and pivoted to face Samir full on. He whispered to her, "When I tell to run go as fast as you can into the woods."

She moved closer behind him.

"Now I don't suppose you are going to shoot an unarmed man, are you?"

"Out here who would know? I might consider just wounding you enough to stop you so that I can complete my plans but then again I might not," smirked Samir. "Come over here my dear if you do not want me to shoot the both of you right here, right now. Step away from him and join me here," he said pointing to his side.

Hoping that the gun had been emptied of ammunition, Bosher lurched forward at Samir, grabbing him by his shoulders. Samir wrestled away and when he found that in fact, the gun would not fire he retrieved a knife from his side and pierced Bosher deeply into his side.

"Run! Run! Kila." Bosher shouted.

In one deft move, he stepped to the side, threw his shirt off and into the face of Samir, temporarily blinding him. Kila ran into the woods while Bosher and Samir fought each other. Blow for blow they tussled onto the ground each wounded and each determined to win. Taking a deep breath in between blows, Bosher mustered all his strength and delivered one final blow to the midsection of Samir. He followed it up with a kick to his right side and a powerful elevated foot kick to the back of his right knee. He pummeled him consistently until he did not move.

Samir was down. In a mangled mess, Samir tumbled to the ground. Bosher stopped when he noticed that apparently when Samir fell, he did so in a fashion that not only broke his neck but the right arm that held the gun.

Bosher was wounded. He hesitated momentarily and then took off to find Kila. He found her wandering in the woods and redirected her so that together they headed for the Canaan Center. As it turned out Jezreel and Zadok separated their troops, cordoned off the children safely and surrounded the thirty adversaries. Once they had them in a crossfire, knowing their weapons were useless, they closed in on them rapidly disarming them and tying them up sufficiently. On their way to the Canaan Center, they turned in the marauders to the local officials for proper prosecution.

Once the marauders were jailed, they returned to get the children settled into the center under the apt guidance of Libi. Not seeing Bosher she asked, "Did Elder Bosher, Senior Priest of Jubilee, return with you?"

"Not yet, He returned to rescue a little girl we missed. I'm certain he's alright," responded Jezreel. She looked piercingly at both Jezreel and Zadok. "How certain are you sir?"

They turned to face her square on, and Zadok said, "I'll go. She's right. He might need help."

Zadok dashed off immediately, moving through the brush and stock of the woods. He was intently focused on Bosher and returning with him safely to the center. He did not want to face Libi with any other outcome. He heard footsteps in the distance and stood still. He camouflaged himself by lying in the grass between two large trees when he heard voices that sounded familiar.

"It's okay Kila. You are safe now, and your brother Seth is waiting for you."

"Am I going somewhere that is safe? Are those awful people going to come for me again?"

"No! I can assure you that where you are going both you and Seth will be quite safe."

Hearing his voice, Zadok stood slowly and identified himself. Bosher was so grateful to see him feeling that he might not have the strength to make it back because he had lost quite a bit of blood from the knife wound. Noticing the bloody clothes, Zadok retrieved a scarf from his pants, tore it and tied it about his side as a tourniquet to minimize the flow. He took a flask of water from his pouch and gave it to Bosher to drink. He placed his arm securely under his shoulder to support and steady him as they trudged on. Bosher had lost a lot of blood, and he was very weak. He leaned heavily on Zadok until they saw the shadow of lights gleaming from the center.

They crossed the threshold when Jezreel and Libi saw them. Jezreel ran to assist them, and together he and Zadok carried him inside and got him onto a bed. Within minutes medical staff was at his side. After attending to Kila, Libi returned to the hospital.

"How is he?" she asked.

"Pretty weak! He lost a lot of blood", responded Jezreel. "He's in a very weakened condition and needs a lot of care and rest."

"He's in the right place. I will oversee his medical regimen personally," answered Libi.

"Nurse! Please get someone to wash him up, change his clothing and dress his wound. He will need a lot of water and aloe immediately. Also, when he awakens see if he will eat something lite and nourishing. I'll be back in an hour to check on him."

Chapter

Medical attention was administered quickly–people were all over him executing Libi's orders quite precisely. Jezreel and Zadok stood by for a while in case he needed to be moved. Once they determined that he was secure they returned to their platoons. They had to take exact measures to ascertain that the center was secure from attack.

Bosher slept for three days, waking intermittently to sup and take meds. They successfully stopped the bleeding and managed the wound, but he was not out of danger. Libi looked in on him throughout the days. He had a glimpse of her once or twice or was he dreaming? He felt soft, yet strong, warm hands pressing a cool cloth on his head. He smelled sesame seed oil and recalled that someone was rubbing it onto his legs while massaging the tight muscles. Someone was consistently applying a minty cucumber smelling substance to his face and arms. In and out of consciousness he sensed the caring presence of a woman in the room and then…out again.

She ministered to him for days and nights. She slept in the room on a cot so that she could tend to his recovery. Although he was in and out of consciousness, she had fresh flowers brought into the room daily so that it smelled heavenly. She had staff wash and oil him in lavender and rose oil daily. His linen was changed daily after exercising his legs and arms so that they would not stiffen. His window was left open just enough so that a fresh, clean breeze could circulate the scents in his room.

Slowly, ever so slowly, he began to recover. He was able to eat a bit more and stay awake longer and longer. "Libi, when can I see him?" fussed Seth.

"Soon. Very soon now. The one thing we don't want is to tire him out."

"Okay" pouted Seth. "But I hope it is soon. I cannot wait to thank him for rescuing my sister Kila."

"I promise to let you know when he is strong enough to have visitors."

Ten days. Ten days after his arrival at the center's medical unit Bosher was able to be transported to a chair. He sat up with assistance and was able to take a deep breath and hold it for a bit. He was grateful to be conscious and aware of his surroundings. He missed praying. It was strange since he had been so out of touch, but he missed talking to God. He tested his memory on one of his favorite proverbial sayings. *"Oh! We should not be mindful to pray that we should have easy lives. Our prayers should request that God will make us stronger people. We should not ask that our assignments, our ministry be aimed and matched to our gifts. Rather, we must pray for strength to complete our assignments. If we are able to pray in this manner, we will not consider the completion of the assignment as a miracle – we will become the miracle. All of this occurs in your spirit by the Grace of God."*

He closed his eyes and breathed deeply taking in the scent of lavender and roses. *"Thank you, Lord for allowing me to assist in the rescue of those precious children. Thank you that we were able to honor our promise to Seth for his beloved Kila."* He took a nap in the chair, and when he awoke, there he was.

"Bosher! Bosher! I thank God you are well." Seth hovered over him smiling. "Bosher! Thank you for rescuing Kila. She is here with me because of you. You kept your promise."

Bosher lifted his head and was overjoyed to see the young lad standing before him. At ten years old Seth had experienced life at the level of a thirty-year-old man. He had lived in hiding caring for his younger sister for years. They had seen their father killed and their mother carted away as a slave. The two of them were constantly running for their lives, from place to place, trying to escape capture or certain death only to be finally caught by the ferocious marauder soldiers.

"Seth. Young man, I am delighted to see you. You're a sight for sore eyes, and I literally mean very sore eyes. How are you? How's Kila?"

"We're living here at the center with Libi. She is taking good care of us. Kila is getting good care also. She totally stopped speaking soon after she arrived here. They told me she would speak again but that she has been so hurt and experienced such trauma that she shut down."

Bosher was quiet and then said, "I believe in a loving, compassionate, caring God who is more than able to calm our minds and hearts so that she will be able to speak again."

"I have heard of your God Jehovah while I have been here and I am eager to know more about him."

"I will see to it, my little friend. Be certain to know that I will be praying ardently for both of you."

Libi stepped into the room and said, "Okay, Seth. You've seen him and if he wants, you'll be able to come to see him again very soon."

"I want. Let him come as often as possible without disturbing his educational program."

Seth smiled and held out his hand. Bosher took it and covered it totally with his. Their eyes met, and an immediate bond was sealed between them. Seth returned to class and Libi ordered Bosher's lunch.

"Think you can stand to eat some sumptuous chicken with seasoned rice, hummus, and veggies today?" she asked.

"I'm starving. Can you add some fresh bread to that menu? Have any fresh grape juice?"

"Oh my! I see your appetite is returning. That's a good sign. Of course! I'll see to it right away." And without hesitating, she left the room.

He hadn't been able to thank her for such wonderful care before she left. She was a whirlwind of energy–a bounty of light that was always moving, moving, moving. Seemingly within minutes, she returned.

The smell of well-seasoned food filled the room. She pulled over a small table and set the tray down for him to dine. She poured a fresh glass of grape juice for him and prepared to leave the room.

"Can you stay and have lunch with me? He asked.

"Thank you, but I only brought enough for you."

"Then can you sit, for a minute, and talk to me?"

She stopped, thought for a moment and then sat down. "How are you feeling today?"

"I'm doing much better thanks to you. I don't believe I would be this far along if it were not for you. Please allow me to extend my deep gratitude for your unselfish sacrifice."

"Just doing my job. No special thanks required."

"Oh, I think that more than special thanks is required. Do you keep watch day and night for everyone? Do you spend sleepless nights of care for all? As compassionate as you are –I think not."

She blushed and fidgeted pulling at her skirt. "Well, you are not everyone. You sir are second in command in the priestly order on Jubilee. You are a renowned, well-loved priest and elder and the beloved of the High Priest Zar himself. Although you slept, Zar has been here several times to pray over you and check on your progress. It is obvious that you matter greatly to him."

"Really! We are the best of friends, and we share a genuine love and respect for each other. Is that why you stayed throughout the night? Was it because of Zar's relationship with me?"

Libi was not a timid person. She could not have maintained such excellent care and control on the children if she had been reclusive in any way, but she was not prepared to respond.

"No. That was not the reason. I just felt led to stay close by, and so I obeyed "The Call." Surely you, of all people can understand being guided and motivated under the provocation of the Holy Spirit."

Bosher managed a huge smile and said, "Most definitely." He thought to himself, *"She's good, very good. But I will explore her motivation further at a later time."*

"Will I see you later? Perhaps, you will consider having dinner with me since I'm still ordered to relax and take it easy a bit more."

"I can manage that. See you around five o'clock" and then she was gone.

He was sleepy, so he put his feet up and rested in the chair. He thought of her. She was about five feet six inches tall, medium to slim build. He assessed that she had dark brownish red hair that she kept wrapped and gathered at the base of her neck. She worked all day with food, children, and medicine, so she carefully kept her hair covered. Her hands were slim yet average size. He recalled their warmth and softness. They were strong hands able to handle many tasks. Her feet and toes seemed perfectly crafted to fit her shoes comfortably because they carried her swiftly, very swiftly, wherever she needed to go. Deep black almond shaped eyes sat perfectly beneath long plush eyelashes and lengthy brows. Her cheeks were elevated just a bit and housed a pair of the deepest dimples he had ever seen. Her teeth were white and fit comfortably under a full mouth. Her lips had a hint of pink that set just inside her bottom lip and peaked out every so often when she spoke.

She wore something, he was uncertain of just what the scent was, but it was perfect for her. He always knew when she had been in the room because that scent lingered for quite a while after she had gone. She was light on her feet and scurried about doing something all the time. Clearly–he was impressed with her and looked forward to dining with her later.

Chapter

Nineteen

Thwarted! It seemed his plans to become the High Priest of Jubilee were thwarted. He had to regroup and try something different. Getting onto Jubilee was a paramount portion of his plan.

Although he missed the ceremony and installation of priests, he had completed the program and officially became a priest without an assignment. An administrative opening was posted on Pruvia—one of the Triune Islands that abutted Jubilee. Apparently, there was a station on Pruvia that processed all applications for those who sought residency in Jubilee. Residential quarters were established on Pruvia during the application period. The screening process was quite lengthy as residents were being examined. Applicants had to attend classes on the rules that governed the island understanding of the Torah and Mosaic laws, background checks into character development and the like. Conjointly, Pruvia also had a holding station for violators of rules, those who had been excommunicated from Jubilee and non-citizen visitors. The current opening was for an administrator to oversee these operations. Natas decided to apply. At least it would get him close to Jubilee and then…He rubbed his hands together and began writing.

Dear Sir: I am honored to be able to appeal to you for consideration of the current opening for an Administrator on Pruvia. A current perusal of my current vita will highlight my management skills which were acquired in a family owned business that I was significantly involved in developing and to date is very successful.

Further, I have traveled extensively and gleaned military experience rising to the rank of Nagad while abroad. Additionally, I most recently graduated from the School of the Prophets with high honors. I am able to follow the rules and regulations succinctly; a trait I picked up as a skilled athlete in school as a youth and later on when competing on the winning team at the School of the Prophets on the mainland.

I am eager to meet with you to discuss the parameters of this position and be able to discuss with you those skills that I possess which make me the perfect candidate for the current opening in administration. I anxiously await a favorable response from you.

Sincerely,

Natas Dephile

Signed, sealed and posted; it was on its way. He stared out the window musing over his options. "*Hmm. You may have won the battle Zar, but the game is not over.*"

He called the Temple Secretary and made an appointment to meet with the new High Priest. The secretary asked for his name, and he responded, "I'm an old friend who went to The School of the Prophets with him. I've been away on a mission and am returning for a brief stay. I'd like to surprise him and give him a good old fashion School of the Prophets salute. The meeting should take no more than twenty-thirty minutes." Joyfully, she scheduled him for two o'clock on Thursday. She told him that a temporary pass would be available for him Thursday at eleven o'clock under the name of

Natas Dephile. "Thank you so much. I hope to get a chance to meet you at that time" Natash said gleefully.

Promptly at eleven o'clock on Thursday, he retrieved the pass and proceeded to Jubilee. He was precluded from entering the city but rather was escorted via the outer road to the Temple for his two o'clock appointment. The guard waited until he was ushered into the outer office for his meeting with Zar. He did not have to wait long before he heard the door begin to open. Zar entered and stood perfectly still.

Natas jumped to his feet and bowed ever so slightly in recognition of Zar's position.

"Zar! You look great! Being the High Priest suits you well. I know you're shocked to see me, but I simply had to humble myself and come to you man to man and apologize for my rude and abhorrent behavior. I've had a few months to review my actions in light of all we were taught at The School, and I came up short. My character lacked a lot of luster. Can you forgive me?"

"Just what are you asking me to forgive you for Natas?"

"Just about everything. I've been selfish, jealous, covetous; you name it. Being an only child, I was used to getting my own way. I had a lot to learn, and unfortunately for me, I had to learn it the hard way. I'm truly sorry for my horrific behavior. I'm here to repent and ask for forgiveness."

"I can't forgive sins. You know that Natas. Have you prayed and asked God to forgive you?"

"Yes! Yes! Absolutely! That is why I am here. I've prayed, and now I have to set aside my pride, humble myself and ask you to forgive me in order to be totally absolved of wrongdoing."

"Okay then; consider it done. I don't hold onto anger. It does me more harm than good. No harm, no foul-we're good", with that Zar stepped forward stretched out his arm and shook hands with Natas.

"I wish I had time to hang around and talk, but I'm really busy today; still getting settled and all. Let's try to get together soon."

"Oh! Yes. I fully understand. I just wanted to see you face to face and conclude this matter. Thanks for your understanding. I'll check with you at another time." Natas turned to go.

"Congratulations Zar! I'm certain you'll be an extraordinary High Priest good for the islands. See you later."

Outside the office, Natas patted his leg and smiled.

"Hmm, wonder what that was about?" Zar thought. *"For sure, Natas is up to something. Can't wait to tell Bosher about his visit. Heads up-game on."*

Chapter Twenty

"*So much to do*" thought Marta. "*What should I take? What to give away? Should we build or look for something already there?*" She decided to make a list and follow it in order to get more organized. Since it would be a while before the house was ready, she had to leave some items in place for Nathaniel's comfort. She figured until everything was finalized Sanu and Jehu would be hustling back and forth between the mainland and Jubilee also. Then, there was Sierra to consider.

Whenever Zar had time and was on the mainland, he managed to cordon off some time to come to the house and speak with Jehu, and the boys and of course see Sierra. She knew her daughter was quite smitten with him and who could blame her? He was an extremely appealing man both physically and spiritually–a man of good character. She continued packing, placing things into piles as she moved about the room when Sierra entered.

"Oh! Please let me help you with this. It is much too much for you to do alone. Why didn't you let me know you were doing this today?"

Marta laughed. "Darling, you spend more time in a trance now-a-days such that much of what I am saying goes right past you. I wonder why that is?"

"Mother, please! I'm so anxious about him. Do you think that things are working out? He's so very busy. I don't know if he has time for me."

"Oh! Believe me, he has time for you, but he has a new position and many challenges. As the High Priest of Jubilee if you are going to have a future with him, you must understand that God is his first love and that people will always have a need for him. Can you stand that kind of a relationship? You know Sierra, you are used to having the full attention of everyone in this house. If you and Zar develop a deeper more committed relationship, it will not be so. I believe he will love you deeply, but the "Call" on his life is one that requires a full commitment to God and service to others."

"Yes. I have thought of that, and I know it will be different, but he is the kind of man that I have prayed for, and I believe that I will adjust well. Plus, you and father, Nathaniel and Sanu will be living on the island also. I am certain that I love him mother and somewhere deep inside of me although he has not said anything, I believe he loves me also."

"Dearest, he is saying he loves you every time he steps away from his office to visit you. Every time he walks through our doors his eyes begin darting back and forth looking for you, and when you enter the room, I can see him take a deep refreshing breath of air. He loves you, and I have a feeling it will not be long before he makes that abundantly clear. Now, please help me sort through these things so that we can expedite our move onto the island."

Sierra hugged her mother tightly and then moved to sort through the items in the room. She stopped for a moment to consider their conversation then smiled, turned and went to work all the while she hummed a happy little ditty. "*Jubilee.*" she thought. She liked the sound of that and looked forward to beginning her new life there.

CHAPTER Twenty-One

"Good morning Monave. How are things going with the shop?" Jezreel asked.

Pleasantly surprised she answered, "Quite well thank you. How nice to see you. You're usually so busy with your guards. You look well. By the way, how did you like those pastries I made the last time you were here?"

"Did I like them? Unbeknownst to you, I've had two of my guards come in here and purchase several of them for me. I ate so many of them I had to do an extra mile running up the mountain to work off the extra weight I picked up."

"Oh no! Are they too fattening? I'll have to adjust the recipe to compensate for that."

"Please! Don't change a thing. I'll just have to be more temperate with them– they're delicious!"

While they were talking Havi rounded the corner and stood to look at the biggest, blackest, boldest dog he had ever seen. Jet was extremely impressive with a huge chest that had only one small crest of white mid-center and one on his right paw. He sat close, next to his master peering around the room taking in all of the sights and sounds. When Havi appeared, he looked down quizzically but did not move. Jezreel touched his ear which meant that he was to keep still and maintain his station.

Havi circled the huge dog trying to assess just who and what he was. He decided to step on his tail–and so he did. Jet did not move. Havi decided to take his favorite toy and put it in front of him. Jet did not move. Havi picked up the little toy seal, shook it with his mouth and put it down in front of Jet as though to tempt him to try to get it. Jet did not move. Havi came right up to him and sat just under his chin and panted.

"Havi! Leave the dog alone. Stop taunting him."

"Don't fret," said Jezreel. "Jet won't move unless I indicate that he is to do so. He probably is trying to figure out just what Havi is" and he chuckled.

"He's an absolutely beautiful dog. Is he yours?"

"Definitely! He's my friend and true companion. We go everywhere together when I'm on watch and even when I am not."

"Well, Havi seems to be quite stricken with him." They began talking again while the two dogs sensed each other.

"Well. I better get going. Just thought I'd stop in and check on you. Umm, you don't happen to have any more of those little sweet tarts, do you?"

"Actually, I made a fresh batch just this morning since they are going so well in the shop. I'll get a few for you."

When she left, Jezreel looked down at the two dogs and smile. *"What an odd pair of companions."* He thought. He reached down and ruffled Jet's fur and said, "Good boy! Good boy Jet."

"Here you go. There are several of them in the bag for you. I hope you enjoy them."

"Thanks. How much do I owe you?"

"Please consider them a gift. Perhaps you will share one or two of them with the guards, and it will encourage them to come in and purchase more."

"Thank you. I'll be certain to order them...I mean I'll ask them to come in and purchase these sumptuous little treats. But I will not share even one of them with those guys. Come on Jet. Let's go."

Jet immediately responded and stood up ready to move out. Havi could hardly believe it. Jet towered over him. He looked at Jet and went over to him and deliberately stepped on his paw. Jet looked down, as though to scratch a flee, stared at him, turned and in so doing swished him with his tail. Havi yelped joyfully and pranced alongside him as Jet and Jezreel left the store.

"Seems Havi thinks he has a new friend. Bring him around again. Have a great day!"

Once outside, Jezreel found that his hand had instantly gone into the bag and that somehow, he had a plump little tart in his mouth. He bit down while Jet looked up. "Oh! No. These are not for you my friend. Let's go we have recon to do on the west end." They headed out for their new assignment.

Chapter Twenty-Two

"I can't believe it! It is simply too good to be true," shouted Mingo. He raised his hands while twirling about and hopping back and forth on his two feet. "God is good. He knows the secret places and deepest wishes of our hearts." He had always wanted a full opportunity to put into practice some of the designs he had on paper and in his head. He had shared some of them with his friend Sanu, and now he had the chance of a lifetime. Together they would build an empire and create ships that the world would seek after.

He ran over to his desk and pulled out his portfolio of plans and began looking them over.

"Perfect." He thought. He paged through a number of his designs. *"This one is too good, swift, yet economical to move product. Yes! This one is ideal. Sanu will love it."*

Jehu and Sanu found the perfect spot to build the manufacturing site. Close to the water near the pier. The elders and Zar approved the facility after much discussion about the design, purpose, and plans for the future. They discussed having minimal effect on the natural habitat and culture of the island and came up with a design that would blend perfectly with the makeup of Jubilee. In addition to the physical design of the facility, the landscape around it would leave plenty of trees and shrubs and invite those strolling along the seaside to sit on the benches that would be strewn along the coast for them to rest on. It would not be noisy or have offensive sights or smells.

In fact, the pattern was very inviting, and those who were curious would be invited into the lobby to glean a better understanding of the manufacturing model. School children interested in engineering, manufacturing, drafting and design concepts would be encouraged to visit the facility and learn more; they were set and ready to go. They would be breaking ground in two weeks.

Jehu had a surprise for Marta knowing how anxious she was about the move. He had found the perfect residence for them, and with a bit of remodeling, it would be the ideal site. He couldn't wait for her to see it and review the plans for the home before he purchased it. She was arriving in the morning along with Sierra. He and Sanu left for a meeting with Zar; they were having a simple dinner together at a new seafood restaurant in town. He had grown very fond of Zar.

They met and welcomed each other warmly just before they sat down.

"I'm starving," said Sanu.

"You're always starving son," said Jehu. "Seems this is the place. Everything looks good and smells appetizing. Although nothing beats your mother's cooking."

"You're right about that, but this just might take a good second."

Zar listened to them chatter and then interrupted when there was a lull. "I'm glad to have this quiet, solemn moment with the two of you. First, I'm so happy that you have had the plans for your new facility approved. I think that it will be a great benefit to the island for employment and future development. Secondly, I hope this is not too soon, but I would like your permission to further my interest in Sierra, and I'm asking for your permission to seek her hand in marriage if she will have me."

Sanu smiled and sat quietly waiting for his father's response. Jehu stopped eating, put his fork down, wiped his hands and then turned to look at Zar. "By now you know how extremely valuable and well-loved Sierra is don't you?"

"Yes sir. I do"

"You know how she is cherished in this family?"

"Yes sir. I do."

"I have but one question for you since I know that as the wife of the High Priest of Jubilee she will be well provided for. And that question is this: why do you want to marry my precious daughter and what makes you think that you are deserving of her?"

Zar was a bit taken back but not too surprised knowing the deep familial relationships that were entwined in their family. He knew that Sierra was more than Jehu's child, more than his only daughter they had an extremely tight bond of love that encircled them–in a very special way they were yoked together. He cleared his throat.

"I don't know if I will ever be deserving of her, but you can rest assured that I will never stop trying to be deserving of her. As you know I am the High Priest of Jubilee and with that comes a tremendous responsibility, however that does not qualify me for being her husband. I have no doubt that I will be able to take excellent care of all of her needs financially; she will want for nothing. I have been well educated in the Law, and I have a specific call on my life to serve God. I will never relinquish that position to another human being, but outside of His primary preeminence in my life, she will be next. Sierra is a beautiful woman, but that is not why I love her. She is brilliant, fearless and spirited; none of these things are enough for me to ask her to marry me. Her beauty far exceeds her outer appearance. She has the heart and compassion of a saint; she is lovely and loving, and I desire to be her covering. I can never take your place sir, but I will try for the rest of her life to make her smile, to share my heart and soul with her and to willingly, if need be, to lay down my very life for her. I can think of no other woman that can fill the warm spot in my heart that only a wife can touch. I have spent careful time with God and asked Him to approve my request for her as a wife. She is my heart's desire, and He has answered me specifically that she is the one He has chosen for me."

Sanu sat fixed and quiet. Jehu rose; the full stature of his being looming before this man who was asking to marry his Sierra and opened his arms to him. "Who am I to interfere with what God has approved? Welcome into our home son."

Sanu stood to his feet. "Whew! You guys are much too dramatic for me. I can't stand all of this emotion. Zar, you are now my brother, and I am ever so proud to welcome you home."

The people in the restaurant stared at them wondering what was happening. The three of them looked around, laughed, paid the bill and left arm-in-arm together.

"Now," thought Zar, "I have to find the right time, place and the right words to solicit a Yes! from the only one that truly matters. God will give me the words of that I am certain."

Chapter Twenty-Three

Jezreel was very proud of the condition of the island and how his guards assured that the grounds around and about it were well maintained. He went on a daily walk with Jet checking on the pier conditions and the inner city of Jubilee. Jubilee was of primary importance to him for many reasons.

He and Jet headed out for the west end of the Island after their brief visit with Monave at the shop. He smiled to himself thinking about her and the way she twittered about doing one thing or another. He was very taken with her, but today he had to concentrate on his new assignment. Something was worrying Zar and Bosher about the development of the west end, and he intended to do a thorough inspection of it. Being assigned to the west end was quite an honor, and he determined to live up to the expectation that he could handle whatever developed. He knew that having Batu as his second in command was the perfect coverage for the inner portions of Jubilee.

He and Jet set out for the farthest end near the cliffs. They roamed all over, and he noticed that Jet was apparently disturbed about something. He was antsy and unusually curious as he rooted about. He always gave Jet his head on these types of missions because he knew that Jet was fit for finding things that were out of order. Jet pranced up and down along the cliffs; he wandered down a bit onto the side and looked back for Jezreel. Jezreel responded, "Go ahead Jet I'm following. Go on boy." And so, he did. Carefully, very carefully Jet eased down the cliffs and landed on the beach. Jezreel was right behind him. Both of them were in a heightened sense of alert. Nothing escaped their eyes. They poked everywhere knowing that something was out of sequence.

They checked the shore for debris, and that is where they found it. A small piece of a shirt that had been torn off was undulating with the waves having been caught between two rocks.

"Hmm…now how had did that get there?"

Jet kept moving along the shore until he found what seemed to be a piece of a bone which had no meat on it but it was a bone nonetheless. He retrieved it and brought it back to Jezreel.

"Yep. I'm with you Jet. Something is mighty strange. None of this should be here. Let's keep looking."

They kept searching, poking in rocks and moving driftwood and ocean debris around and then they found it. About two hundred feet below the upper portion of the western end of the cliffs were signs of movement. Plus, it seemed that a few large boulders were strewn together haphazardly against the land. The shore signs were unnatural; the boulders were randomly placed against the land as though they were covering something. The rocks were too big for him to budge alone, but he knew just how to fix that problem.

"Come on Jet let's get some help with this. You were right ole' buddy; you found the problem again. What would I do without you?" He patted his back and rubbed behind his ear as an affirmation of good behavior. They climbed back up and quickly called Batu to come down with six of his guards. He was going to find out what was behind those rocks and he was going to find out today.

Chapter Twenty-Four

Bosher returned to Jubilee and rendered an excellent report on the Canaan School to Zar and the Elder Committee. They were well pleased and spoke of adding a similar project on the west end of Jubilee. Not the whole concept but perhaps just a small extension of the school and counseling center since a medical facility was already in the planning stage. Plans for the western development of the island were projected to begin in a few weeks. He had a lot to do, and he knew just how to begin.

"So, what do you think Zar? Do you agree that she would be a great addition?"

"Yes. I do. I'm very impressed with her. Are you?"

"Well of course I am. She's an excellent counselor, a great nurse, well prepared and a well-schooled instructor and she is totally dedicated to the well-being of the children. What else could we ask for? She is sensitive, caring and compassionate, warm and affable, extremely experienced in caring for children, she's…"

"Okay, okay, Wow! I'm sold and apparently, so are you."

"What do you mean by that? I'm convinced that she is a perfect fit."

"That's obvious, but the question is perfect for what?" He winked at his friend slyly.

"Oh, come on. What are you trying to infer?"

"I didn't infer anything. I'm just wondering if you are aware of how obviously enamored you are with her."

Of course, he knew, and it was apparently very clear that he could not hide it from his friend.

"Okay. I'd like her to be on the island so that I can pursue these feelings I have for her which is very hard to do with her on the mainland and me in Jubilee. Plus, she is the ideal candidate for the job."

"Well my friend, get to it. Try to seal the deal as quickly as possible because if she agrees she'll want to be in on the development of the Canaan School extension. Do you want me to send another delegate over to speak to her about it?"

"You are a horrible man! A horrible friend and for the first time, I have noticed that you have developed quite a sense of humor at my expense. No! I'll leave in the morning to speak with her."

As promised, he left in the morning for the mainland. He called ahead to let them know he was on his way down and that he needed to set up an appointment with Libi for early evening.

When he arrived at the school, everything was in perfect order as he expected. Unknown to him Seth was waiting for him when he walked through the door.

"Bosher! Bosher! I've missed you, and I am so happy that you have come back to visit so soon." Seth rushed up to him and stood there beaming all over. Clearly, he was glad to see Bosher.

"Seth. Come over here and give me a hug. How's Kila? Is she speaking yet?"

"Not yet. But I've been praying for her voice to return and I know that it will."

"Praying? To whom are you praying Seth?"

"Jehovah of course! Libi has been teaching me about Him as well as counselors and elders in the school. I'm a full believer Bosher. I know who He is and why I must serve Him."

Bosher looked at the young lad before him, and his heart swelled with pride. Seth was no ordinary ten-year-old; he was special, and Bosher had grown very fond of him. He liked him a lot, and he was committed to assuring that he had whatever he needed to fully develop into a man after God's own heart.

Libi entered the room and stood there peering at them. "Okay young man. I know that you sneaked out of the counseling session as I expected you would, but you must return plus I have a scheduled meeting with him."

"Okay, but don't leave without saying goodbye. How long will you be here?" asked Seth.

"At the most, two days I have to return to Jubilee immediately."

Libi moved closer and invited him into her office for the meeting. Once there she asked,

"To what do I owe the pleasure of my boss so soon?"

"Your boss? I was hoping that after having taken such good and personal care of me, you would at least consider us friends."

"Yes. I do consider us friends, and for the record, I am glad to see you doing so well."

"Thank you, but I have a specific mission, a special professional purpose for this meeting that I would like to discuss with you." She lifted her head and asked, "And just what would that professional purpose be?"

He shifted a bit in his seat, "Libi, the High Priest and Elders Counsel on Jubilee are developing the west end of the island to include an extension of The Cannan School, and we would like you to become the director and oversee the full development. We are offering a really good salary, which includes independent living quarters and full administrative autonomy."

"My goodness! And if I consider this offer when would you need me to leave for Jubilee?"

"As quickly as possible; we are breaking ground on the foundation of the school in a few weeks, and we would like your input on the final design."

"I'm very interested, but I cannot leave here without making certain that I have staff in place to carry on the work we have here."

"We are prepared to assist you as best possible with that. Will you consider the offer?'

"Who would I be reporting directly to?"

"That would be me. I am the elder assigned to the west end."

"Oh! Okay, then the answer is no."

"Why? Why Libi? I will not interfere with your duties at all" he was very alarmed.

"I'm just kidding. I am very pleased to have been considered for the position, and I am honored to accept it with the understanding that I can complete the things I need to take care of here."

She was smiling, and he was totally embarrassed by his response. She had a sense of humor and was extremely witty, and she knew just what to say to him; just the right way and when. He tried to compose himself quickly and said to her, "Well then it is settled. I will leave tomorrow after breakfast, and if you give me your immediate needs, I will see to it right away." He stood to leave.

Quietly and softly lowering her voice and the intensity in her eyes she said, "Bosher. Thank you for considering me for the position. Thank you for being my friend. I am looking forward to the challenge and will give it my very best. I look forward to living in Jubilee, and I look forward to making new friends there."

"Count me among those friends. You are perfect for this position. It's all you. If you can give me a list tomorrow, I'll move on it immediately. And don't worry about assistance with moving. I will send some of the guards to assist you."

"Thank you. See you in the morning."

Chapter
Twenty-Five

"Well, what do you think? Isn't it perfect? Not too large but just the right size for us and the changes in our lives with the children. Here's what I'm thinking." Jehu moved around the room sweeping his hands in the air painting imaginary fixtures and rooms in the air. "Yes! And right here I was thinking to develop the kitchen and cooking area so that it will be ultra-modern. The pantry will be just off the kitchen right here which will be on the other side of a door going to the outside where I will build a fresh herb garden for you. What do you think?"

She loved it when he was engulfed with creating things for her. He got so excited and was so intense about making certain that everything matched perfectly and was to her liking. It was one of the ways that he expressed his love for her since building and creating things with his hands was a comfortable means of communication for him. She trusted his judgment totally and would have affirmed his decision without looking at the property. He was right on it. She loved her home on the mainland, but this…this was exceptional. The whole island was an expanse of beauty; a magnificent unprecedented distinct natural splendor. The sights, sounds, and smells were beyond explanation. Jubilee was an island that bespoke of a majestic veneration of nature. She was pleased-very pleased with the home and the site he had chosen for them.

"Jehu, you have outdone yourself. It is magnificent! I love the ideas you have expressed, and I can't wait to get started. I think I'm really going to love living here. When can we move in? I don't mind a bit of discomfort while we shape our new home together. In fact, it can be quite exciting and a bit of an adventure. Plus, I really miss having you at home or at least near me."

That was the final touch. He knew she liked it when she added that sweet little bit of endearment at the end. She always did that when she wanted to convince him of something.

"We can move the things from the house into this place immediately. It is large enough to handle everything, and we will simply move items around as necessary. I'll have our bedroom furniture and Sierra's placed in the appropriate rooms immediately and purchase temporary bedding for Nathaniel and Sanu here until their bedrooms are ready to be permanent. So, if you want to return home and expedite things with Nathaniel's help, we can get started right away. Perchance by the end of this week, we'll be in the house. I've already made the proper business connection to seal the deal for the sale of the home and land and just wanted your approval."

Sierra wandered into the house just as they finished their conversation and without uttering one word, they knew that she liked it. They shared the plans with her, and she nodded that she was eager to get started with the move. She and Marta would return to the mainland in the morning to finish the last vestiges of the move. "Did you see that gleam in her eyes?" said Jehu.

"I certainly did. In her mind, she's looking at what could possibly be her new environment with Zar. I think she is quite impressed with the house but far more enamored with Jubilee and him." They winked at each other knowing that Sierra would not be long with them especially since Zar had already voiced his intentions of marriage to Jehu.

Sierra and Marta left in the morning for the mainland and the excitement of a new life, a new environment and a culture that was warm and inviting while it was growing and developing into a renown cultural and spiritual center. Both of them in their own dynamic ways had much to contribute to it, and they were eager to begin.

Once he saw them off, Jehu signed the papers for the new home and the additional land that was adjacent to it. Then, he called Nathaniel to get the ball rolling for the move and explained to him where they were with the purchase of the home and the development of the new business building. In turn, Nathaniel told his father about the challenges of moving the business to Jubilee and his responses to those challenges. Jehu was pleased with his son and knew that he could handle all of the sundry decisions that would go into making a smooth transition. He paused for a moment in the room and thought, *"My family is growing and developing. God has blessed us immensely. Soon Sierra will be married to Zar who is the High Priest of Jubilee, Nathaniel will take his rightful place in the company with a promising future, Sanu will have the opportunity he has always wanted which was to express his creative side more prominently and Marta, my Marta will be close to all of them and I will be home with her much more."*

"Father, words cannot express my gratitude to you for all of your multiple blessings. Just a season ago, I was in a deep quandary and deep spiritual challenge and because I chose to follow "You and Your Way" you have extended yourself to me beyond the health and happiness of my family and stretched Your mighty wings over my whole life. I have come to trust you in all things, talk to you about all things, big and small, and you never fail to answer me." Slowly he sat down, picked up his Bible, turned to Psalms 139 to read the thoughts that David penned which exemplified his sentiments completely.

"**You have searched me, LORD, and you know me. You know when I sit and when I rise: you perceive my thoughts from afar. You discern my going out and my lying down; You are familiar with all my ways. Before a word is on my tongue You, LORD know it completely. You hem me in behind and before, and you lay your hand upon me. Such knowledge is too wonderful for me, too lofty for me to attain. Where can I go from Your Spirit? Where can I flee from your presence? If I go up to the heavens, you are there; if I make my bed in the depths, you are there. If I rise on the wings of the dawn, if I settle on the far side of the sea, even there Your Hand will guide me, Your right hand will hold me fast."**

Tears slowly pooled in the corner of his eyes and slid down his cheeks as he continued to read. The final passage ended with…'**when I awake, I am still with you."**

Reverently, he closed the book and sat quietly thinking of the multiple blessings God had bestowed upon him. Ever so slowly he arose, lifted his hands and his eyes toward heaven and whispered. "Thank You!"

Chapter Twenty-Six

Ashima was blindly in love with her husband. He was everything she had ever dreamt of and more. She stretched and yawned in the huge bed to get ready for the day. Batu had been on night duty for a couple of days; she wondered why he had been so pensive so secretive about his new assignments, but she knew better than to pry too deeply. She bounced out of bed, showered, washed her hair with the new scent she purchased from Monave's shop and began to prepare a fulfilling breakfast for him.

She moved swiftly around the kitchen, setting the table, preparing a fresh glass of juice and mixing the ingredients for fresh soft biscuits which were his favorites along with eggs, seasoned chicken, a few salmon strips, banana oatmeal and a bowl of fruit. Batu was a big guy with a big appetite especially when he stepped up his training schedule in preparation for an assignment. She wondered again what his assignment was but did not stop to waste too much time on it; he would tell her when the time was right.

As quiet as a mouse, he eased into the kitchen and swept her up in his arms, spun her around, messy apron and all, and then placed her gently back on the kitchen floor.

"Oh! Batu you are such a tease. You know I had my back to the door, and I was busy making breakfast for us. Not fair."

"Life is not always fair sweetheart which is why I am constantly asking you to keep the doors locked and to be alert at all times. Even here on Jubilee life is changing a bit."

"What do you mean? Aren't we still safe?"

"Of course! The Trinity Islands are probably the safest place on earth for you. Our militias are trained in every defensive maneuver imaginable plus. However, as the island grows, we do not have a benchmark on life here since we are growing so quickly. Please, just keep your wits about you at all times."

"Okay. Are you hungry? Is everything alright? You haven't said much about your new assignment on the west end yet."

"Don't worry your pretty little head about that. There's not much to tell yet, but I will include you as I learn more. Something smells delightful. Is it ready? I'm starving."

"Wash your hands and sit down; everything is ready for you."

He smiled thinking about how adept she was in the kitchen. *"Pretty, witty and a great cook. I have a great wife!"* He washed his hands, wiped them and sat down to dine with her. She always set a spectacular table and this morning was no exception. They talked while they ate and he helped her clear the table before he left the room. He was tired after such an arduous night. He asked her if there was anything, she needed him to do before he took a brief nap. She responded that she needed him to move a plant and a chair but that it could wait until much later. He sat in his chair, took off his boots, laid his head back and within mere minutes he was peacefully asleep.

After she cleaned the kitchen, she quietly peaked into the bedroom to see him sleeping while sitting in his chair. *"That's strange. He usually lies across the bed. He's sitting there as though he might need to leave quickly at any moment. He and his troops have been really pressing hard with training. I know something is up but what could it possibly be? Hmmm. Knowing Batu, he'll be on top of every situation."*

She placed a lite blanket over him to quell the chill of the morning air and eased out of the room.

Chapter Twenty-Seven

Within a week of his visit, Libi notified Bosher that she would be prepared to leave the mainland for Jubilee as soon as he let her know that all was ready for her entry. He advised that he would have several men there to assist her with her move in two days. When they arrived, she had everything arranged properly, she said her farewells to the staff and her friends the night before, and she was off after one last visit and farewell.

Seth entered the room quietly and sat down next to her. She faced him squarely and prepared for the hardest part of her departure. Before she could speak, he went close to her and said, "I know you're leaving for Jubilee. I've heard about your big promotion and the big opportunity for you there. I'm very proud of you, and probably there is no one better to handle and work with the children than you, but I will really miss you." Tears filled his eyes as he tried to smile. She grasped his shoulders and pulled him close to her. She stroked his hair, his face, and shoulders and rubbed his hands in hers.

"Nothing will ever happen to ever make me leave you and Kila. I am going away for a brief moment, and as soon as I possibly can, I will send for the two of you. Do you believe me?"

He shook his head affirming that he did as he wiped his eyes.

"Seth. I will not abandon you and Kila, but I must go and make a safe place for you to join me. I do not know much about what I am going to encounter, and at least here I know that you are in good hands and that you are safe. Can you understand that?"

"Yes, I do. It's just that I know that we are safe when you are near to us. I can relax when you are here and I…am still a bit frightened when I think that marauders could take us away again. I have to keep Kila safe. I think she is beginning to relax a bit and I expect that she will begin talking again soon. I am praying that she will speak again. I miss her voice. You and Bosher are the only people that I trust with Kila and me."

"Seth. I know Bosher gave you his word that he will not let anything happen to you. I trust him. Do you?"

"Yes. Yes, of course, I do."

"Please continue to pray for us and for your safety. I know you are safe here at Canaan. Kila is making great progress here with her teachers and counselors, and I do not want to disturb her routine. I will be back and forth checking on you both until I can get you into the new school on Jubilee. You can always reach me by phone; I will always respond to you."

He hugged her tightly and pushed back a bit from her. He squared his shoulders and nodded that he understood, he kissed her cheek and turned to leave the room.

"Libi, thank you for everything that you have done for Kila and me. Without you and Bosher I don't know what would have happened to us." He lowered his head and closed the door behind him.

She looked out of the window and thought, "*I knew it was going to be hard but…this is much too painful. I love them deeply, and I think that this is the best way to proceed. I want to take them with me, but*

I have no legal authority, no permission, nowhere to house them or know what I am going to encounter."

"This is best." She threw her shawl over her head and one around her shoulders and went to meet the men Bosher had sent to assist her. She found them standing in the foyer of the school ready to move out. They had all of her belongings packed on the truck ready to go. She waved a last goodbye to her staff and friends and went off to find her way on Jubilee Island.

Chapter Twenty-Eight

He couldn't believe it; he was actually pacing back and forth. He was so anxious for her to start her new position on Jubilee. Her new quarters were not fully completed, but he had made arrangements for her to live with Marta and Sierra for a brief moment. He hoped that they would become friends which would make her stay somewhat smoother. He, Marta and Sierra gathered early in order to meet her at the dock to welcome her to Jubilee. She seemed genuinely delighted to see him and to meet Marta and Sierra. She and Sierra were about the same age and appeared to hit it off quite well at their first meeting.

Marta and Sierra had much of the house arranged comfortably while all of the adjustments and additions were being made. As it turned out, she and Sierra decided that they would get to know each other better as they explored the Trinity Islands more and especially the western end of Jubilee. Libi was given her own room and a private bath in order to make her stay as comfortable as possible. She fit in quite well and jumped in immediately to assist with making preparations for lunch. She and Sierra were chatting all the time as though they were old friends; he was very happy about that. Marta took to her instantly in a motherly way and melded into their conversations intermittently just as though they were her two daughters.

Jehu, Zar, Bosher, Marta, Sierra, and Libi all gathered for lunch at the home of Jehu and Marta. Zar immediately went over to welcome her to the island and to express his utter delight that she had accepted the position at the newly created Canaan School. He informed her that they were prepared to incorporate her ideas into the design that had been drafted and hoped to get started the first thing in the morning. She remembered him well from his visits with Bosher when he had been injured. She was still very impressed with him and looked forward to her new position with total enchantment. Jehu was probably one of the biggest men she had ever seen but instantly knew that he was a gentle giant especially when he was around his family. She felt extremely welcomed and comfortable and eager to see the rest of the island.

Bosher and Zar had planned an extensive tour of the island with Sierra and Libi after lunch. As they concluded the meal, they all prepared to stretch out for an adventure while they all got to know each other a bit better. Because much of the west end was still undeveloped, they decided to charter an open horse and carriage in order to be able to take in all of the sites up close. It was a beautiful day coupled with temperatures in the mid-eighties, a lite breeze, clear skies and huge, fluffy, puffy pearly white clouds as they set out for their adventure. A perfect setting, for both young ladies as an introduction to Jubilee.

"Oh, my goodness," said Libi, "this Island is unimaginably beautiful. It is the full expression of allure and loveliness."

"I totally agree," chimed in Sierra, as she reached for Libi's hand. "It is seemingly flawless. I am certain we will love it here."

"Jubilee is certainly the most beautiful of the three islands, but there is so much more. Mount Mizaan has an ambiance all of its own. It is the summit of spiritual distinction and will totally capture and consume your attention when you venture there. The smallest of the three islands–Pruvia is extremely nice also and has a specific purpose in maintaining the balance of all three islands. We'll take you there at another time as we will for Mount Mizaan also."

Bosher joined in, "I fully agree, Zar. Each of the islands has a unique quality associated with it. The Trinity Islands is a full blend of utter delightful, peaceful living experiences. Our ancestors planned well for its continuance leaving a well-marked path for us to follow."

Chapter Twenty-Nine

After a brief nap, Batu arose, strapped up his boots and began to prepare to leave the house. He kissed his wife good-bye and promised to return home as soon as possible later that day. He went into the closet to retrieve his rain and wet gear, threw them into a bag and left.

Storm was Batu's special friend; his private dog assigned specifically to him. No one touched him; no one gave him orders but Batu. It was understood that Storm belonged to Batu Kadesh. He had been trained from birth to accompany him on tours much like the other dogs in the garrison. They had a special bond, a special language that they knew when communicating with each other and it worked very well; they were a unit.

Storm was Jet's big brother. They had been born to Ram, his father and Ebo, his mother in a litter of five puppies. Storm was the oldest and mirrored his father to a tee. Ram was huge with a big chest, gigantic paws, strong, straight spine, thick fur and bright eyes that were constantly looking about. Storm was a chip off the old block. Big and robust just like his father. His gait was even and strong, his back was perfectly erect, his fur was thick and well defined, and his eyes were piercingly bright and alert. There was no question that he was the son of Ram. Jet was the youngest of the male puppies and took after his mother, Ebo. He was black all over except for a crest of white fur that was center of his chest and another patch on his right paw. He was a very healthy dog with good energy, quick wit and a delightful sense of humor; he was a bit playful yet very smart like his mother, Ebo. The litter had been carefully bred for service to the guards. They served their masters well.

Batu entered the barracks, went straight to the kennel and signaled for Storm to come to him. Storm knew that he was in the barracks and stood ready for him to open the door so that he could join him. They looked at each other momentarily, and together they turned and left the barracks. Once outside, Batu reached down to pet his friend and checked that all was well with him. He tweaked him on the nose, chucked him on the jaw and rustled the fur on his head. Storm swept his tail back and forth several times to indicate his utter delight in being with Batu.

"We have a very important assignment Storm. Seems your brother Jet has found something awry down at the western end of the island. Let's join them." They trotted off and jumped in the jeep to quicken the pace to Jezreel and Jet. Once they got there, they scurried down the rocks to the bottom and joined Jezreel and Jet at the place where the bone and clothes were found. Batu saluted Jezreel and looked at Jet admirably while the two brothers circled about while playfully nudging each other.

"He's just like his big brother. Sharp! He definitely found something that needs to be investigated."

"I'll say. This bone and that shirt should not be here. I couldn't move the boulder by myself. Did you send for more help?"

"What? You could not move that big, huge, boulder by yourself? Have you been skipping your weight training?" Batu threw his head to the side and laughed.

"Yes! They should be here shortly with gear to move that boulder, so we can get inside."

"Great. Let's take the dogs and walk down the beach to see what they can discover."

"If there's anything out there those two will find it. Storm! Let's go, boy."

At their cue, the dogs jaunted off ahead of them as though they had been talking. They poked everywhere, smelling and digging around the perimeter. Storm leaped ahead and began pawing at a spot feverishly. Jet joined him, and the two of them began barking for Batu and Jezreel to join them. Without hesitating, they ran to where the dogs were located and immediately became alerted to some type of entryway. Traces of movement of something heavy were imprinted in the sand and scratches were etched into the rocks. Together Jezreel and Batu began moving the stones away one-by-one until they made a hole big enough for them to crawl through. Once inside they found just what they needed to know. Without a doubt, someone had been on the island. They found evidence of a half-eaten piece of fruit, a bag of clothes and a large box of ammunition conveniently covered and set aside on a rock platform. There were no markings to indicate who they belonged to, but it was certain they did not belong on Jubilee.

Clearly, someone was planning a siege operation. For what reason, they did not know, but one thing was certain–it would not happen in their lifetime. Instead of going any further into the cave they decided to turn back and meet up with their troops to determine what was behind those huge boulders. Storm and Jet were eager to press on knowing something else was ahead, but they obeyed and left with their owners without delay.

They did not have to wait long for once they turned the corner, they found the troops standing at the ready for them. They had all the equipment needed to move the boulders and had already begun the process. They pushed several of them back and entered the portal only to find an assorted array of artillery, ammunition and militia type weapons. They took quick inventory being careful not to disturb anything; they did not want to alert the culprits that they had been discovered. They assessed everything and turned to leave as they had come being careful to replace the boulders as they had been found. They decided to caucus above in the plains of the west end.

When they had assembled above, they huddled together and agreed that there was no question that someone was planning an attack on Jubilee in the near future. They drew a map on the ground of what they had found and hatched a plan of recourse and attack. They decided to station a small platoon on Mount Mizaan to determine when they were coming and going and where they were coming from; that would begin immediately. Three men quickly retrieved their gear and left on that assignment. Jezreel and Batu planned to leave and returned to the center of town to report to Zar and Bosher. The rest of the platoon stationed themselves around the west end so that they were out of sight on a twenty-four-hour tour.

"Jet! Storm! Let's go!"

Chapter

Thirty

"Sierra, I would like to take you on a tour of Mount Mizaan tomorrow if your father will allow it. I thought that perhaps Bosher and Libi would like to join us. Would you like to go? Do you have time tomorrow?"

"Why yes. I am very curious about Mount Mizaan and could think of no one else I would like to tour it with than you. What time shall I be ready? I'm certain I can talk Libi into it also."

"I'd like to get an early start there's quite a bit to see. How about nine o'clock?"

"Perfect. Shall I pack a lunch?"

"If it is okay with you, I have that all taken care of. I am delighted that you have agreed to accompany me there. I'll pick you all up at nine o'clock. Please be certain to tell your father of my intentions and that you will have company other than me."

"Okay. I'll do it right now. See you tomorrow."

She hung up the phone, almost tripped over her own shoes and ran into the living room to get her mother and Libi. "Mother! Mother! Come in here I have something to tell you and you too Libi. Hurry up."

They dropped what they were doing and hurried into the living room to find out what she was so excited about.

"You'll never guess what just happened. Zar just called and asked if he could take me on a tour of Mount Mizaan. He made sure to ask me to advise father and get his okay, and he plans to have Bosher and Libi go with us. Is it okay? Please say that you will make Father say that it is okay. Libi, will you go with us?"

Marta and Libi looked at each other and laughed out loud. They shook their heads and hugged each other. "My dear child, I would be considered the most heartless mother in the whole world if I did not agree. Surely, if I hesitated, you would break apart right here and now. Of course, I am certain that your father will agree especially since Bosher and Libi will be with you." Libi swiftly moved to her side and hugged her. "I think that man really likes you. I think that you have etched your way into his heart, and he has special intentions to make you his own."

She giggled and threw her skirts in the air as she twirled around.

Nine o'clock sharp Zar and Bosher approached the house, after checking each other over twice and smoothing down their hair and beards. The girls were ready to go. Jehu opened the door and welcomed the gentlemen inside. He shook hands with each of them and gave Zar a special sly wink and smile.

"Okay gentlemen, you have precious cargo here so handle with care. Will you all join us for dinner later?"

"Yes sir," said Zar. "We'd be delighted to dine with you and the lady of the house."

"Then off with you all. Have fun." Marta and Jehu waved to them and then closed the door.

"Think it will be today?" Marta asked.

"Yep. I'm pretty sure of it."

The day was simply perfect for a trip to Mount Mizaan. Bright, sunny with clear skies; a pristine island day. They crossed over in a comfortable boat and landed on the pier of the island. You could immediately tell that there was something serene and wonderful about the environment there. There was something special about the island ambiance that made you feel light and free; whole, perfect and complete. Zar and Bosher had planned so that they would each take the ladies on a separate special, personal tour and then meet back on the pier at an appointed time for lunch in the picnic area. Zar helped Sierra as they strolled down a path while he pointed to all the foliage, animals, and the ocean shore as they toured the island. He took her a bit higher with each round of the mountain making certain not to tire her out too quickly.

"This is where I come for my personal retreats; my time of refreshing and talking to God. Here is where He talks to me and guides my steps for the people of God. I get my marching orders and directions from Him on this mountain. Mizaan means spiritual balance, spiritual refreshing, rejuvenation and intimate time with Him. On several occasions, He has called me to the top of the mountain, and I have had an opportunity to commune with Him as I suspect Moses did and as He did with Samuel, Paul and others during their seasons of leadership. I dreamt of speaking to Him all of my life, and when my opportunity came, I wished I could have melded right into His arms forever. I wished I could have gazed upon His glory forever. It was more than any words could express." She listened carefully and then looked at him and said, "You actually heard the voice of God? You actually knew that He was speaking specifically to you? He actually called you to come up into the mountain?"

"He did, and I did."

A look of awe and amazement covered her face. "Zar. How very special you must be to Him."

"Sierra, we are all very special to Him. I am loved no more or less than you. I have simply been charged with a special assignment that I utterly cherish. Make no mistake about it. God is no respecter of persons; all of His children matter greatly to Him."

She was quiet and pensive, and her gaze lingered long upon his face.

"One of the reasons I brought you here was to introduce you to a place where I spend a lot of time. I come here for relaxation and to talk to God about issues and concerns. The other was to speak to you about something that is pressing on my heart. I am certain that by now you know how very much you mean to me; how much it matters to me that you are happy and that all is well with you." She listened quietly yet intently while staring into his eyes.

"Sierra, I have spoken to your father and brothers about my intention to ask you to consider being my wife and they have given me permission to approach you on the matter. I'm not very good at this sort of thing, so I'm a bit off base but… it would be my utter delight if you would just think about, just consider accepting me as a candidate for marriage. You don't have to answer me now, but I would like it if you could at least let me know if there is a favorable chance of acceptance."

She motioned for him to help her up onto a small rock platform which was nearby. She wanted to be a little taller than normal. He stretched out his hand to take hers and in so doing totally swallowed her whole hand in his. She grabbed onto three of his fingers, and he assisted her to the platform. Once there she balanced herself and turned to him. However, before she could speak…

"I imagine that you are not ready to marry so soon since you are so young and beautiful. Not to mention, you have just recently moved here. It's just that once every eligible man in town is aware that you are here there will certainly be a rush to impress you with their skills and talents and they may sweep you away from me before I have a chance to let you know how much I love you. You would not have to worry about being taken care of or living in the style that you are accustomed to; I will provide for your every wish and concern."

As big as he was, as strong as he was, as much appeal and impressive power that was his as the High Priest of Jubilee, he seemed vulnerable and pliable and open to her. It was obvious that he was nervous–quite nervous.

She motioned for him to come closer to her and he did. When he was within reach of her, she placed her small hand in the cleft of his chest and then positioned a tiny finger just left of the corner of his lip. He stood still and waited. Even while standing on the platform of rocks she was still not up to his shoulders, but she lifted her head and spoke to him.

"Please relax. We are together here in your favorite place. My whole heart answers you with a resounding "Yes." Although I have not had the benefit of actually speaking to God directly as you have. I do have a very personal relationship with Him also, and He has confirmed to me that you are my husband. I simply had to wait for you to ask and as hard as it was, it was well worth it to hear you utter the most precious words ever spoken to me. You need to know dear, that there is no one else that comes close to you in my mind. Are there any other men in Jubilee? If so, I have not noticed them for they are overshadowed by the presence of you in my heart and mind. I cannot wait to be your wife for I know within my heart of hearts that I am your rib, your wife for life. Thank you for asking me to be joined with you as a wife married to the most dynamic man on the whole island."

Passion swelled within him and he ever so gently bent down and kissed her. She returned the kiss with her own thrust of emotion, and they embraced there on Mount Mizaan. He released her, took her hand in his and helped her down.

"You have made me the happiest man on earth today. I pledge to you my heart and my commitment to you alone. God has blessed my heart beyond my wildest dreams by providing me with a woman such as you. I am so delighted that your family has come to Jubilee because in all truthfulness there will be many times that I have to be away from home. I come to the mountain several times a year as necessary, and I travel to the mainland also. The duties of High Priest are extreme and can be trying at times. Do you think you will be able to withstand the stress and challenges associated with being the wife of the High Priest?"

"I can withstand whatever is necessary to be your wife. Whatever I don't know I will learn and if you promise to be patient with me as I learn the responsibilities associated with your position, I promise to be an eager student and make you proud of me."

"You are more than I ever expected. We'll be fine together, and I look forward to presenting you as my wife. In all honesty, I must say that I hope we can set the date soon because although I am the High Priest, I am very much a man and I am so moved by your mere presence that I think it best to try to move it along in order to resist all temptation. I am used to keeping myself under control, but when

I am near you, it is a pressing challenge that I do not know that I can withstand for long."

She giggled and squeezed his fingers. "I know what you mean I feel the same. We can talk to my parents when we return if you would like."

"Yes. Let's do that. Come on it's about time for us to meet up with Bosher and Libi for lunch."

They casually made their way to the pier area and the lunch table and began preparing the meal made for them. They talked all the way laughing in between and nudging each other occasionally. She was so animated, and he was so reserved and calm. He listened to her banter and smiled to himself knowing that he had received yet another blessing from God. He knew that a man was supremely blessed when he was able to find a good wife that he loved and cherished more than himself.

Bosher and Libi were not far behind them and entered soon after them. They were all aglow and eager to share the stories of their adventures on the island. Zar and Sierra listened intently and smiled as Libi and Bosher spewed forth with all of the sights and sounds they found on the mountain; they simply loved it. They ate a sumptuous meal and settled down for a bit until Libi said, "We've totally taken up all of the time talking about our adventures. How do you like the island, Sierra?"

"Oh, I liked it just fine. Zar asked me to marry him."

"What?" Libi jumped up and ran around the table and hugged her friend until she almost lost her breath. Sierra hugged her back, and they prattled on about one thing and another as though the men were not even there.

"Congratulations Zar, You finally did it. I knew you would eventually get around to it. Was it really hard? I mean, did you choke or cry or fidget until she guessed what you were trying to say, or did you just come out with it?"

Zar punched him lightly in the arm and hugged him. They were brothers, and he knew that Bosher understood him better than almost anyone else. "She was merciful with me and took pity on me and said yes early on." He gave up a huge smile and patted his friend on the back.

"I'm happy for you. You deserve the best. Whatever you need I'm here for you as always."

"I love you, Bosh. Please keep us in your prayers."

"You are never out of my prayers. Know that it is done."

After lunch, they parted for a short while. Zar took Sierra up a winding trail and across a small meadow which faced the ocean then down a slight incline. Once there he covered her eyes with his hands, and when they were perfectly still and pointed in the perfect direction, he took his hands away. She gasped when she saw it; for right in front of her, just a few feet away was the most perfect house she had ever seen. It was not merely the house but the whole scenic appeal. The ocean swept onto the shore like an adept dancer careening through the air in a perfect leap of joy. The sand was a peachy melon like white that was filled with little flecks of crystal blue highlights and chips of shells mixed perfectly together while puffs of filtered ocean mist bounced against the shore. Together; air, land, and sea embraced at the shoreline in flawless unison. She was amazed by the splendor of it all.

"Zar…this is an absolutely flawless beauty. Is it yours? Is this where you stay when you're on the mountain?"

"No. I had this built for us. I prayed so very hard to find the right gift, the perfect wedding salute that would capture how I feel about you and God gave me this vision. I have never slept here because I wanted to do that with you for the first time to make it our home. I wanted something permanent and special that was worthy of you– my soon to be wife. This site includes the house which has three bedrooms and a kitchen, two full baths, laundry facility, etc. Also, it has a separate stable which is off to the right a short distance away. Can you see it?"

"Zar, I have no words, I can hardly believe that you did this for us, for me. Oh! It is awesome!!! Can we go down and enter it?"

"Yes. But I prefer to enter when we are married. I want to cross its threshold as man and wife. I want to christen this home with a special dedication that only the two of us will engage in. However, if it will make you happy, I will take you down there right now."

"No. Your way is much better, more serene, more special and spiritual. We can rightly baptize this home on the first night that we are married, just the two of us away from the world communing with each other as a unit. Then, we can ask God to bless it and us in a very personal way." She squeezed his hand and put her head on his arm as she leaned in next to him.

"However, I have one more gift for you which we can go view right now if you want."

"I want. Can we go now?"

"Right this way young lady. Be careful, take my hand."

They walked together down a small pathway to the stables. He opened the door, and there stood two of the most elegant horses ever seen. He asked her to stand still a moment and then released her hand and moved toward the stable. He entered and returned with an extraordinary golden palomino horse specifically for her.

She stood 15.1 hands high. Allure was a phenomenal golden palomino with a full mane of glossy white hair that was also sported on her tail. She was absolutely beautiful with huge deep brown eyes, satin smooth skin and a personality that was gentle yet definite. Allure lived up to every iota of her name. She was indeed charming; bobbing her head sending her stark white hair flowing around her neck in an array of fluff and glamour while her pure white tail swished and swung in tandem. She was enchanting and seductive in an equine sort of way, her eyes were huge and engaging, and she pranced high as though she knew that she was exceptionally beautiful. With all of this, Allure had a personality that was soft and gentle. She was eager to prance around showing off her rider as one who was fitting to mount and ride such an exquisite animal.

Sierra moved slowly towards her running her eyes over her from head to toe. She reached out her hand to touch her and Allure bowed her head as though she welcomed the warmth of Sierra's hand. Sierra moved slowly around the horse and then held Allure's face in her small hands staring into her huge dark eyes. Right then and there–in that very moment horse and rider were bonded. In that very instant, they knew that they were a perfect meld; a perfect match and they were both delighted with the decision. Allure was hers, and Sierra was totally committed to Allure.

"She's beautiful! She's the perfect gift. Thank you! Thank you for loving and caring for me like this. I will try to make you a good wife,

I will commit to us and to the mission that God has for you...for us. I love you, Zar. I totally love you."

"You are more than welcome. I knew when I saw her that she was the only choice I could make for you. She emulates who you are in her stance and mannerisms. I am delighted that you like her. Now, I would like to introduce you to her stablemate; my horse Koach."

"Is he in there?"

"Oh yes! Koach owns the stable. Koach is full force and power as his name indicates. He is exquisite in a different sort of way than Allure. You'll see. I'll call him. Koach, come boy! Come."

From an expanse of darkness that filled the stable came the biggest most awesome horse, she had ever seen. He came to the brink of the stable door and looked around. He nodded his massive head in recognition of his owner and then stood perfectly still until Zar motioned for him to come closer. Slowly he picked up one leg at a time as though to profile himself for her to view. He stood a menacing 16.3 hands high. Koach was a flawless, pure white stallion who manifested pure white unpigmented skin and abrupt, sheer white hair on his mane and tail accompanied with deep, dark brown eyes. Power and force; Koach was power and force personified in a huge pure white stallion. It took a while for him to settle down, but now, he belonged to Zar. He knew it, and Zar knew it. Zar spared no expense in caring for him.

"I thought that when we came to our special retreat here on Mount Mizaan that riding these two would add a special dimension to our time together. Carrying the weight of the Islands and being the High Priest is a tremendous amount of responsibility and I need quiet time and replenishing quite often. I come to the mountain for spiritual rejuvenation, rest and relaxation. I hope we will spend many wonderful, memorable days here."

"I never imagined my life with you would be so enchanting. I only pray that I will enable you to know the kind of love you deserve. You are so generous, and you deserve every good thing."

"Sierra. I belong to you; never forget that. Hold on to it because I will be away from you quite often. Know, without a doubt that there will never be anyone else for me. First God and then there is you–Sierra, my only love. I willingly give myself to you, I will always love you. And you sweet Sierra, are my always. But…let's get out of here this is too much for a man to stand. Let's run back to the pier. Are you ready?"

"Absolutely! Surely, I can outrun you." With that, she lifted her skirt and took off running. He looked at her momentarily and thought *"Oh! This is going to be fun. Life with her will never be dull."* Then, off he went jogging quickly behind her.

The trip back to Jubilee was filled with fun and laughter. The two couples mingled well together. Zar and Bosher just looked at each other as the ladies chatted on and on from one subject to another. Once they reached Jubilee, they slowed down a bit, just long enough to check on their respective partners, and then picked up exactly where they left off. As they got closer to the house, they slowed down a bit and took their places at the sides of their partners. Sierra opened the front door and called out for her parents.

"Yes. We're here in the kitchen. Are you alright? Have fun?" said Marta.

"Oh! It was spectacular! What a day! Where is my perfect father?"

"Perfect am I," said Jehu as he entered the room. His eyes shifted left and met those of his wife. He smiled, tilted his head and asked, "Just what makes me so perfect today little lady?"

Silence, for what seemed like an eternity until Marta said, "Come sit down for a moment so you can all tell us about your day. Dinner will be ready shortly."

On demand, in unison, they all sat down. "Well, what was your day like?" asked Jehu.

No one spoke. Jehu and Marta looked at each other quizzically.

"Everybody okay?" Marta piped up.

Finally, Zar stood up towering over everyone except Jehu. 'Today sir, I asked Sierra to be my wife, and she has graciously agreed. As you know, I did consult with you first, and today I spoke with her, and she said yes."

Silence. Marta and Jehu looked at each other then stood up together. "Finally. Finally, we can breathe again. Finally, we can stop wondering when and how and if. Welcome into our family son. If you didn't ask her soon, I was afraid that we might find her in a melted puddle in the garden one day having fretted herself to death." Jehu roared with laughter at his lite hearted joke.

Marta moved to hug her soon-to-be son and then turned and lingered awhile gazing at her only daughter. She kissed and hugged her a long time and then she whispered in her ear, "he's perfect for you. Be happy darling. God bless you both."

Jehu swept her up into his arms effortlessly, as he had done so many times when she was a child. He hugged her and kissed her cheek until she said, "Father! I can't breathe." He gently put her down and turned to shake Zar's hand.

Dinner was aghast with wedding chatter and the tour of Mount Mizaan and future plans and the island home he had built for her as a wedding present. Joy. Total blissful joy filled the room until late into the evening.

Chapter Thirty-One

"Yes sir! We'd like to meet with you and Elder Bosher as soon as possible. Yes sir! We'll be there first thing in the morning."

Jezreel hung up the phone and turned to Batu to report the conversation. They agreed to meet at the pier at 7:00 A.M. to go over their report findings. After their brief discussion, they gathered their gear, took their respective dogs and left.

Batu returned home to Ashima who was preparing what was obviously going to be a sumptuous meal from the smells emanating from the kitchen and the clanking of pots and pans as he entered the house.

"Oh hi! You startled me."

"Why?"

"U*h oh!*" thought Ashima. "Oh! Just because I was totally immersed in thinking about how to prepare this recipe for dinner tonight. I wanted it to be special cause I thought you'd be really hungry when you got home." She turned to face him with a soft, warm and lovely smile on her face.

"Ash, I have asked you several times to make sure that you keep the door locked especially when I'm not home. I have explained my reason several times, and yet you still manage to leave it unlocked which, I might add, is why you were startled."

"I'm so sorry. You have asked me to do that, and I continue to forget, but I promise to make it a habit. You look a bit tense. Everything go alright today?"

"Yes. Everything is fine but I might have to be away from home for a while on a recon assignment, and I need to know that I can trust you to keep the doors locked. In fact; while I'm away I want you to either stay with your parents or have Deja come and stay with you. What do you prefer?"

"You're scaring me. What's the matter? What kind of reconnaissance?"

"You know very well that I do not talk about work when I'm home. It is nothing that is prone to injure me; it is just that we need some essential information."

"What for? Information about what?"

"Everything smells delicious, and you were right I'm starving. I'm going to clean up and then I'll be back to spend some time with my favorite girl. Let me know what you want to do when I leave. Your parents or Deja to come here?"

He left the room quickly with her staring after him. She sensed something different in him, something ominous but she knew her Batu. He was resilient and determined. Whatever it was or whoever it was would face an awesome foe in Batu Kadesh. She picked up the potholder and began turning the ingredients to what promised to be a lavish meal.

In the meantime, Jezreel took Jet back to the barrack and got him comfortable for the evening. He patted him and rubbed him for quite a while letting him know how proud he was of his performance that day. Jet soaked it up. They both knew that they had challenges in front of them that promised to be revealing. After he left Jet, he headed to Monave's shop.

"I love the way this place smells. Have any of those sweet little pies you make?"

Monave turned and smiled at him. "How nice to see you looking so strong and mighty standing there in all of your military attire. You must have been on quite a trip today. Everything okay?"

"Of course. I've got the best troops in the world. Man for man; I'd put them up against anyone."

Hearing his voice Havi came dashing around the corner and stopped just short of his boots.

"Easy little fella. He's not with me today; he's resting. I'll bring him by next time."

Finding that Jet was not with him, Havi gave him a long stare and went behind the counter. "Well, I guess I know who's important to him" chuckled Jezreel. While he was talking about Havi, Monave fixed an assortment of sweets for him to try.

"Here you go, sir. Try these little treats and let me know what you think."

"They're good I know it. You fixed them so they'll be perfect."

She smiled at him warmly. He stuffed two of them into his mouth and made ridiculous sounds of enjoyment as he gobbled them down one after the other. She watched in total amazement as he ate each one of the treats.

"Monave I'm going out on a special assignment in a day or so and I want you to know that I will still have the shop covered, on a daily basis, with one of my guards. I don't want you to be concerned that I have abandoned you for one instance."

"Oh, I'm not concerned. Nothing has happened since that one little situation with the sailors. And you took care of that aptly. When are you leaving?"

"Within the next day or so for what might be a few weeks. I need to be certain that you are okay so a guard will be here or very nearby every day until I return."

She looked at him intently and walked up very close to him. "Jez what's the matter. You never speak to me like this. Are you in any danger?"

"Danger?? Ha! I laugh in the face of danger." He waved his hands as though swatting at a fly.

"So... you are going into a dangerous situation. Will you be alone?"

"No. I will most certainly not be alone. No. I am not in imminent danger. Yes. It matters to me that you are alright. I need to know that you are safe."

For the first time that she could remember they had a serious and somewhat intimate moment. He was saying many things to her without uttering specific words. It was clear that he cared for her and she was totally delighted although quite concerned about where he was going.

"Mo, I have been hesitant to express my feelings for you although you must have sensed my specific concern and care for you.

However, if you will allow me to, I would like to speak to your father about moving closer to you and developing a more serious relationship. I would like to know if you think it possible to return my care for you. Is it possible that you would allow me to see you so that we might determine if there is a future for us? I know I'm always careful not to overstep my bounds but... I really would like to develop a deeper, more personal relationship with you. Will you give me permission to speak with your father?"

"Jez I..."

"Look I'm a big guy. I'm not going to break if it is not a good time. We can remain, friends, until perhaps you'd like to move closer at some time in the future."

"Jez I am a bit taken aback; just a little surprised. I didn't expect you to sweep into the shop one moment in search of little treats and then ask if I would think about us developing a deeper relationship. Truth be told, I've been waiting for you to ask." She uttered a lite chuckle as she said, "I've been feeding you for weeks hoping that I might entice you to want to approach a little closer. Yes. I give you my permission to speak with my father, and yes I am very interested as I have been for some time in developing a deeper relationship with you."

He took a few steps closer to her and looked down to search her eyes a bit deeper. *"She is so beautiful; warm and lovely. I love her smile and the way her shoulders shake when she laughs"* he thought. She stood firm with her heart pounding to a steady deep rhythmic beat and waited. He held out his rather substantial hand, and she placed hers in it. With his other hand, he closed over it gently and said, "I'll be ever so careful to tread lightly so as not to disturb you. I do not want to frighten you with the level of care and concern I have for you. I am very interested in developing our friendship so much deeper, more committed, more specific and personal. I will speak to your father, if he is available before I leave to go on assignment."

Her eyes glistened as she said, "he'll be available I'll see to it. Jez, I might be a woman, a rather small woman at that but, that is no indication of the quality of my feelings for you also of the steadfastness of my ability to commit. I am not frail or weak or so delicate such that I am unable to withstand being with a man of your strength and caliber. I'm looking forward to advancing with you."

"I will call your father this evening and make an appointment to speak with him. Thank you for considering my request."

"I am certain it will be my pleasure. Please don't leave to go away before saying good-bye to me if that is possible."

"I'll make it possible. Can I wait for you to close up? Need me to carry anything home?"

"I'll be just a minute."

Chapter Thirty-Two

Zar and Bosher met early at the Temple office. Zar had apprised him of the application that Natas had made for the Administrator position on Pruvia and of his office visit.

"That guy never gives up. He's always up to something. What are your thoughts?"

"I think it's best to keep him close, so we have a better chance of knowing what he is up to. You can bet he's not interested in being an Administrator on Pruvia. He's full of tricks, treachery, and deception. I could never figure out why. He was born into wealth, has good looks, a great athlete, smart, has skills, talents, and abilities beyond the norm, and it has never been enough. He's always trying to get more by any means possible; always cunning, always mendacious, always deceptive. It beats me."

"Zar, I am convinced that some people are so selfish, so egocentric and narrow-minded that their world only considers their needs, wants and desires to the detriment of everyone else. He's one of those people. He's given himself over to the devil; he's so fully consumed with treachery and deception that he probably doesn't know why he does the things he does himself–consumed by evil; that's Natas. He has chosen the dark side of life on his own volition. After all, he's been to the School of the Prophets and passed with high grades. He knows the principles of God as well as we do if not better. He has simply chosen vile, evil, deceptive ways as his mode of behavior."

"It is troubling none-the-less to see him travel down this road of certain destruction. His heart is full of rebellion. Seemingly he spends time thinking of all the evil he can do to stir up trouble and discontent. The concept of peace and tranquility evades him. Wisdom from the sixth chapter of Proverbs tells us that there are seven things that God hates: naughtiness, lying, murdering, plotting evil, eager to do wrong, a false witness and sowing discord. Natas is guilty of all of these things."

Bosher responded, "Amen and Amen again. It is so sad to watch, but the truth shall prevail in the end. Can a man hold fire against his chest and not be burned? No! Natas is doomed for certain destruction. I agree. Let's keep him up close."

"Deception, tricks, lies, and evil fill his heart. His plan is to take control of that which God has set in order for His glory. Deception will not prevail. There will be a final reckoning in which God alone will rise victorious, and we will be on the winning side."

About an hour later, Jezreel and Batu entered the office; along with them was Zadok because of the quality of his men and his commitment to Jubilee. Very specifically they reported on their findings on the west end of the island. They explained their plan to station men on both Mount Mizaan and at the west end to monitor all activity and to determine how things were advancing. Together the five of them hatched a plan to protect the islands at all costs with as little disturbance as possible to the inhabitants; no one was to be alerted until it was absolutely necessary.

Jezreel, Zadok, and Batu were given total authority to take charge of the plan to protect the islands. Zar and Bosher were extremely confident in their capabilities and that of their troops. Jezreel advised that he and a few of his soldiers would be going undercover in order to infiltrate the ranks of the army that Natas was formulating. Zadok was assigned to find out what he could about any affiliation on the mainland with Natas. He would continue to inform Batu of the situation, but in order to minimize detection, he would only communicate with him. All agreed to the plan, and each set out to execute their respective responsibilities immediately.

Zadok, along with several of his men went into the far reaches of the mainland. They visited several different tribes and cultures all of which were bandits, marauders, and scavengers of one sort or another. If there was anything nefarious going on, they would find out about it by hanging with these heinous scoundrels. They grouped together as though a band to make themselves more appealing and to show strength in numbers.

Jezreel left to gather his equipment and leave for Pruvia. Before leaving he marshalled all of his troops together, revealed the plan and had total buy-in from each party. Some of his young men were anxious and wanted to engage the outlaws straight on. Jezreel took the time to remind them that knowledge was on their side and that an unexpected surprise response would be very effective. He reminded them that victory was certain to be theirs, but beyond an immediate victory he wanted to assure that they would never have to engage this kind of threat again; the young men understood and fully committed to the plan to wait until another day to trounce on their enemies effectively. He explained that in his absence Batu would coordinate all efforts and that they were to give him their total support.

Then, he took his time and slowly dialed the number to call Monave's father, Adarsh. Once he had him on the phone, he asked if it were possible to speak with him later that evening. Monave had already told her father to expect a call from Jezreel and to be certain to make and to keep the appointment. At precisely five o'clock he approached the house, knocked on the door and was ushered in by Cherish who could not help but render a beaming smile that lit up the whole foyer.

"Hello, Captain Jezreel. Welcome to our home. I guess you're here to see my father I'll go and get him" and she skipped off.

Shortly after, Adarsh entered the room and shook hands with the young soldier then, he motioned for him to come in and sit down. The house was strangely silent.

"It is good to see you Jezreel and to know that you are well. You and your men do such an excellent job in paroling the areas here on Jubilee. We all feel so very safe and secure."

"Thank you, sir! I appreciate your gratitude. However, I have come on an important mission today that has nothing to do with my position."

Adarsh decided to have a little fun. "Oh! What would that mission be?"

"I didn't think it was going to be so challenging; I know how he is about Monave."

He cleared his throat and proceeded. "Well sir, I have come to ask for your permission to speak with Monave about us."

"Us? What about us? I was not aware that you and I had any business dealings? Have I forgotten a commitment that I made with you that involves us?" He said this while rolling his hands around in front of him and pointing back and forth between him and Jezreel; all the while, he was totally enjoying watching the impressive captain, a dynamic massive man, fidget.

"Oh! I didn't mean you and me – I meant to say that I would like your permission to speak to Monave about developing a relationship."

"Jezreel you've known Monave since she was a little girl. Certainly, by now you know her and I heard that you actually saved her from two hooligans at the store. I need to thank you for your intervention."

"Oh! That was no problem. Actually, I'm here to speak with you about pursuing Monave in a deeper more personal relationship. You are quite correct I've known her since she was a young girl and now, I would like to see if our relationship could go deeper: be more permanent."

Jezreel patted his brow and whisked away the perspiration that was forming there.

Adarsh took pity on him and interjected. "Mo has spoken to me just a bit about you, however, I am certain that she has bent her mother's ear even more. I understand that you are interested in her and I certainly understand why. She is a unique young lady. She has a very successful business, is a doting daughter and sister to her brothers and sister and she is very involved in the community."

"Yes, I am very aware of this."

"Are you aware that she is very headstrong, much like her mother and that it may be quite challenging to "manage her." When he said this, he raised his hands, spread his fingers, and rocked them back and forth just a little.

"Yes sir. But I am certain that with careful thought and good communication these things can be managed. It is important that you understand that I am not simply enamored with her, I am not overly emotional but rather, I am very deliberate. I have taken my time to speak with her and watch from a distance as she evolved from a young girl into the very charismatic young woman that she is today. My intentions are honest and forthright, and I am extremely interested in investing much of myself into a possible future with her if she feels so inclined. Might I ask what you would require of me to take your permission to spend time with your daughter to determine if she would consider me as a possible husband?"

Hearing the words, Adarsh stood up and faced the young man. When he did so, Jezreel stood also. They looked at each other momentarily and then shook hands.

"Consider that you have my permission. And, consider that you have my blessing for a good outcome also."

He motioned for Jezreel to have a seat and then left the room. When he returned Jaya was with him as well as the twins and his oldest son, Cherish, Havi and last but not least, Monave. They entered the room smiling, and each of them approached him to shake his hand. Havi simply stood at his feet and took one paw and placed it on his boot. Jezreel reached down and patted him on the head. After a brief conversation with her family, they each left the room leaving him with Monave.

"Well you did it, and you're still alive." She smiled at him looking as lovely as ever.

"Finally, we can begin on our adventure together. I am very happy about it. Thank you for keeping your word and speaking to my father before you left on your assignment."

"I always try to keep my word; it is vitally important to me that you trust me. However, I am leaving in the morning on assignment. I will not be in contact with you for awhile since it is a reconnaissance mission. I wish it were not now, but I cannot control that. I did not want to leave without you knowing how very serious I am about us and trying to determine if we have a future together."

"We do," she said assuredly. "We have a very promising future together, and I will be right here waiting for you to return safely. As best possible, please send word to me that you are well as often as possible."

"I'll find a way to do that. Keep your eyes open and your head up because you never know when I will appear." He laughed and moved toward the door. "I must go quickly so that I do not fail to be on time. I miss you already. I miss seeing you scurrying around the shop, I miss tasting your baked goods, I miss your smile and your playful ways and your constant attempt to make people around you happy. I will do all that I can to return home quickly and pursue our future together."

She was silent. She was afraid to express the feelings that were quickly pooling in her heart; she was eager to come out and shower him with full expression. She felt it was too soon and that in time he would know and experience the fullness of her total respect, admiration, and adoration for him. Her eyes glistened as he turned towards the door. Softly she said, "Be safe. Go with God."

He tapped his heart twice, turned the knob on the door and left saying, "I'll be back for you."

Chapter Thirty-Three

The plans for the school were developing quickly. The ground had already been broken, and the foundation was laid. Framing for the walls were quickly being erected, and the flooring for some rooms had already come into fruition. Her quarters were elaborately designed, and she was excited to see the plans advance. Utility lines for the phones, electricity, waste, and water were already in place. Soon, very soon, she would be up and running. Bosher came every day to oversee the project and to see her. She was thrilled at the development of their relationship; she looked forward to her future with him.

Bosher carefully examined the design of the school and the quarters for Libi on a daily basis. Simultaneously, he secretly met with Batu and received a daily report on the activities of the present-day raiders on the west end and on Mount Mizaan. They had a good handle on all of their daily activity, and in fact, their action steps had slowed down considerably. Jezreel and three of his soldiers had already infiltrated the staff of Natas on Pruvia; they were receiving active and on-going reports. He was certain that whatever would come about they were ready to meet it head-on.

"Bosher isn't it beautiful?" Libi was ecstatic with the progress that had been made so quickly.

"Yes. Have you spoken to Seth recently? Have you been able to get away to see Seth and Kila?"

"Actually, I was there for a few days recently to check on them and how the school there was doing. Seth was delighted to see me and Kila hugged me vehemently; seemed she did not want to let me go."

"Is she speaking yet? Has she made any sounds or attempts to speak?"

"No. But she is much more demonstrative; more eager to touch and hug. She seems more relaxed, and she is very affectionate with her brother Seth. He dotes over her, and she is very responsive to him. I love the way they are together."

"Good. I have to get down there to see them. I have spoken to him on the phone recently."

"Yes. He told me, and he was extremely happy to hear from you."

"Those kids have touched the very core of my heart. I am committed to taking care of them."

"As am I. I plan to bring them over to Jubilee as soon as I can house them comfortably."

He was quiet for a moment as he looked around the facility. "Seems we have a lot in common beyond this edifice."

"Seems we have."

"Libi, I am very dedicated to developing this school for you to manage and to looking after both Kila and Seth. Truth be known, I'm even more interested in developing my relationship with you."

"Hmmm. Why Elder Bosher are you indicating that we are in a relationship?"

"Why yes! Don't you know that? If not, I'll have to fix that immediately." He swirled around and faced her and said, "Libi, will you have dinner with me tonight? In fact, will you please marry me?"

Shocked to the point of being unable to speak; she just stood there in amazement.

He seized the moment. "What's that? Did you say Yes? Oh! You have made me the happiest man on earth. When can we set the date? Is tomorrow too early?"

"Bosh! Stop it! Stop it right now! Are you serious? What are you doing? Did you ask me to marry you?"

"I believe you have that right young lady. Yes! Yes! I most definitely did ask you to marry me. I simply am not creative enough to design some other way then to just come right out with it. Libi, will you marry me?"

"Yes! Yes! A hundred times Yes." She stood there with her hands pressed against her face looking so very vulnerable. She loved Bosher. She knew he was the one the very first time she saw him and now here he was, out of the blue, asking her to marry him.

He moved very close to her and took her hands in his. He dropped his voice and took a very serious stance and spoke to her heart, "Libi, will you please marry me? Will you please commit to being my wife tomorrow?"

"Of course, I will but not tomorrow. The whole island will revolt if we do not include them in our wedding plans: soon dearest; very soon." He kissed her gently, held her face and let her go.

Janet Y. Perkins

"Tomorrow. I want it to be tomorrow, but I'll defer to your plans and your timing but make it soon."

Chapter Thirty-Four

Jezreel and three of his soldiers entered Pruvia through an application to become residents of Jubilee as so many before them had done. Because of his prominent position on Jubilee and his desire to be incognito he took time and let his hair grow long, sported a well-shaped beard and wore street clothes indicative of mainlanders and fashionable sandals. His men did the same in order to disguise themselves and hopefully fit in with the other applicants. All of them filled out applications to work on Pruvia in one of the many operations. There were several positions open in the various utility plants, holding cells, administrative offices, food storage facilities, public transportation operations, technology centers, medical hospitals, library operations, etc. Natas had secured the Administrator position on Pruvia and was responsible for overseeing all operations on the island. Zar and Bosher kept a close eye on him from this vantage point. They required monthly and some weekly reports on an on-going basis to be submitted to the Assistant Elder in charge of Operations on Jubilee. In turn, knowing about the report that Jezreel and Batu were giving to Zar and Bosher he made certain to have two sets of eyes on everything. Jezreel and Batu were very clandestine and maintained a low-key manner; they were careful not to be detected.

Jezreel secured a position in the jails and holding facilities in order to be close to Natas. He was certain that it was there that Natas recruited his converts. One of his men was hired in the technology center, another in public utilities and the other in the administration and processing department. They reported all strange and suspicious activity to Zar immediately. Once having the confidence of Natas, Jezreel became a close confidant to Natas and shared in many of his innermost decisions. At first, all seemed to progress well, but as time passed, he noticed that Natas was voicing more discontent with others and himself with how things were being run on Pruvia. Initially, he began by complaining about the salaries he was forced to pay the employees for all of their hard and diligent work. Then, he complained about the quality of the food and the housing on the island as compared to that of Jubilee. All of a sudden, things on Pruvia were highlighted as being inferior to that of Jubilee, and he simply did not understand the reason. Were the people of Pruvia less important than those on Jubilee? Were they less capable of being good citizens? After all, he posed, everyone living in Jubilee had not come from the founding fathers. Why was it necessary for them to have to take training sessions or be introduced to a class on life in Jubilee that was filled with all manner of rules and regulations?

In order to gain more of his respect, Jezreel began asking the same questions of Natas. At first, he just listened to the complaints from Natas and remained quiet. Then, slowly he began asking Natas if he had received an answer from the "Senior Management" on Jubilee to their concerns.

"Why no! They haven't even bothered to respond to me. Isn't that rude? Disrespectful? They want us to learn how to adapt to them, but they don't have to be concerned about how we live and what matters to us. Does that seem fair? Where's the justice in all of that?"

"I don't want to speak out of turn sir, but it does seem a bit unfair. I shouldn't complain because I don't have a recommendation for you."

"Well, I am working on a way to get an answer. Would you be interested in meeting with me later tonight for a special meeting I've organized?"

"Sure. I don't have anything to do after work but rest. What time? Place?"

"Seven o'clock in the multi-purpose room of the Holding Cell facility."

"Okay. I'll be there at seven o'clock."

While he was away from the center and had a quiet moment, he found a secluded corner and called Monave. He missed her and longed to hear her voice.

"Hello. This is Monave. How can I help you?"

"Can you throw me a kiss? Can you shove one of those sweet tarts you make through the phone?"

"Jez! Hi! Are you okay? When will you be home? I'm always throwing kisses to you every day. Don't you feel it? I have a pile of sweet tarts ready for you. When can you pick them up? Today? I have them ready, hot, fresh sweet little pies just for you."

"I wish I could get to them today, but that's impossible. More importantly, I miss your face; I miss the way you smell. I miss seeing your smile and hearing your voice. I'll get home if only for a little while as soon as I can. Will you wait for me?"

"Silly. I've been waiting for you for what seems like years. Who can step into your boots? Of course, I'll be waiting anxiously for you."

"Keep your head up and your eyes open. I'll be home soon. Gotta' go. Please take care of yourself."

She was almost dizzy with excitement over his call. He had the most masculine voice; all deep and strong and oozing with the vibrancy of a man. She was very much in love with him and could scarcely wait for him to come home. She steadied herself and remembered that she was at work and had much to do. Just then, bouncing around the corner of the desk and taking a quick moment to determine just where to find her; he appeared.

"Havi. Havi you always know how I'm feeling. He just called, and he's okay. I think he'll be home soon, and I just know he'll bring your pal Jet around to see you." Havi sprinted over to her and rubbed against her legs and then stood on his hind feet for her to rub him. She picked him up and held him close to her. They had a special moment together and then she put him down.

"I've got so much to do. No time for smooching now. I'll rub and tickle you a bit later this evening."

At precisely seven o'clock Jezreel went to the multi-purpose room as planned. There he found Natas and about thirty other employees gathered around a table with some little sandwiches and drinks. He moseyed over and picked up a sandwich and stood eating it when Natas came over to him.

"Glad you could make it. This is just a little gathering of employees who have the same kind of questions and concerns that you have. Nice people who only want to work for a fair wage and a decent means of living. They don't see a need for all these regulations and classes and reasons to have to pledge their lives just to live on an island. It takes so long for you to get an affirmation and a pass to go to Jubilee. Doesn't seem fair to me; nobody here has a jail record. Nobody has been convicted of any crimes, or stuff like that but…we have to get their approval on just about everything."

"Hmmm. So, what's the plan? How can we change that? We don't have any power."

"Oh! But we do have power. Not from them but the power that we can give to ourselves. We've got a plan which I will share with you a bit later. For now, just relax and get to know some of the men and see how you feel about what they are saying."

"Okay. Looks like quite a crowd; must be thirty guys in here."

"Thirty? That's nothing we have meetings like this going on in two other places also, I bet we have at least two hundred people who work on Pruvia and their family members on the mainland who are just as upset. Soon, we'll have enough to hatch a plan that will have a sufficient amount of power to make a significant statement. Are you interested?"

"You bet. I only have one life, and I want to live it to the fullest. You can count on me."

"Great. I'll keep you informed as we proceed with our goals. Enjoy the evening."

By 10:00 that evening he had given a very detailed report of his findings to Zar and Bosher. In order to coordinate information, they immediately informed Batu of Jezreel's findings.

Chapter Thirty-Five

"Do you think it will work? Do you think that getting married within a month of each other will work?" Bosher asked.

"Of course. It is our wishes that matter as long as we align ourselves with principle. I think it will be really nice. Something different and special and given the alarming circumstances surrounding us with Natas, I think it is perfect. It will give us the time we need with our new brides before the "Happening." Whatever that entails," responded Zar.

"Well, Libi and Sierra are truly excited about it. Both of them are planning their ceremonies together, and I must admit I like the special blessing that will flow from your presiding over my wedding and me over yours. Exceptional and memorable; let's do it then."

The whole island was abuzz with the news that the High Priest was getting married within thirty days of the priest that was second in command. Best friends joined in marriage by best friends. Exhilaration and enthusiasm charged the air on Jubilee, Pruvia and the mainland. Friends and relatives on the mainland ignited in a fury to make arrangements for the weddings. In fact, that is how Natas found out about the wedding and made an appointment to meet with Zar and Bosher. They agreed and decided to gather at the station on Pruvia in three days at ten o'clock sharp.

"How good to see you both," said Natas. "I'd like to give you a quick tour of the things we are doing here on Pruvia."

"Great. We can talk as we walk along."

"This, as you know, is the Admin building where we complete the final processing for applicants approved to go to Jubilee. Everything seems to be going well here. I send you monthly reports, so you know that there are many people interested in residing in Jubilee."

"Yes. We have reviewed your reports which are very thorough. What's that building over there?" Bosher inquired.

"That is the Technology Center where we process upgrades to technology, review data flowing in and out of Jubille, design research and development projects, etc."

Natas took them on the rounds of all of the operation sites on the island explaining in detail each specific assignment. As they completed the tour and were heading back to his office, they passed who they thought was Jezreel simply based on his size and build. He did not look anything like himself with his beard and long hair and different street attire. They passed each other as though they were perfect strangers.

"Well, I guess congratulations are in order for the two of you."

"Thank you, Natas. We're blessed to have found such extraordinary women."

"I'd like to be able to offer my congratulations with a gift. Is there anything either of you would like or consider as special?"

"Please. Do not trouble yourself. There are so many gifts flowing to us that we can hardly take it all in. Just keep us in your prayers."

"As you wish, however, I wanted you to come down here so that I could make you personally aware of a situation I have that is growing here on Pruvia. It seems that many of the employees are concerned that they are being underpaid and have major questions about how and why it is necessary to endure the long procedures to gaining access to residency in Jubilee."

Zar raised his eyebrows, "Hmm. Well, how are you responding to them?"

"Oh! I carefully explain that the wages are fair but that I will make a comparison of like wages on the mainland and give them an update. They thought that was fine and they were willing to wait on the report. Further, I explained that we do not have anything to say about the residency requirements on Jubilee. If we want to reside there, we simply have to follow the rules and regulations and be patient."

"How is that message being received?" asked Bosher.

"Everyone seems calm and understanding. It's nothing to alarm yourselves about I just wanted to make you aware of some of their concerns."

"Well please keep us in the loop. And if you have any dissidents that you find are unruly, as the Administer of Pruvia, you have authority to release them to work on the mainland and quell the whole situation."

"Right. I'll keep that in mind."

"Okay, we'll be headed back to Jubilee. You're doing an excellent job here Natas. If you need anything, please let us know."

They all shook hands and prepared to go to their respective offices.

Zar thought about it, "You'd think everything was fine and nothing was amiss listening to him. It is truly unfortunate that he has chosen this life that is full of absolute deceit and deception. It'll all be over soon. Let's get back to Jubilee and our plans for marriage. We may not have a lot of time before he strikes, and we counter."

"Agreed."

Chapter Thirty-Six

It took a while, but finally, Zadok found the time to contact Jezreel and render his report. Previously, he had managed to send a quick note to say that he was well and that things were progressing as planned. With careful plodding and probing, he was able to connect with an extremely unsavory bunch of heathens who knew that something was going on with Natas and friends on Pruvia. They had been a part of the band that was digging a cave on the west end of Jubilee and storing gun supplies, food and wares for a future run on the island. The band did not know why there was a planned attack on Jubilee, and they did not care; they were paid very well and were told to stand by for future assignments. They were looking for additional support in their mission to further develop the cave for egress and ingress for ease of transport of supplies. Zadok and his men readily signaled that they were available. He advised the leader that they had another job that was quick so that they could make some fast money but would return shortly. He left a number that could be used to reach him should they need to push off sooner than later.

Zadok took his men back to Jubilee for a brief reprieve with their family and friends. They agreed to meet at their rendezvous in three days in order to head back to the bandit hideout. As soon as he got home, he met with Batu, Zar, and Bosher and updated them about his findings.

Clearly, Natas was planning to storm Jubilee using external forces at some time in the future. Zadok did not feel that the attack would be soon since the leader advised him that they were still in need of developing the cave and moving supplies in for his army. Zadok did not feel that it would be long before some sort of affirmative action would be seen, but it would probably be in a few months.

They listened to each other and pieced together a picture that was becoming increasingly clear. Natas was planning something fatalistic; something very sinister. They knew they could handle it because they had been careful not to reveal their knowledge of his plans. They all agreed that they would band together so that there would be little or no bloodshed on Jubilee and hopefully none at all. They wanted to defeat their foes with knowledge, prayer and with the favor of God. They were not anxious about the outcome at all- God was definitely on their side, and they had the confidence and assurance of His support. Zar advised that he was waiting on a word from God to counsel with Him on exactly what he was to do and when.

After the meeting with Zar, Bosher, and Batu, Zadok decided to go home, shower and get a good meal. Prior to that he looked in on the balance of his troops and advised them on the status of his specific mission. They were glad to see him and to know that things were proceeding successfully. He told them about the environment that he was in and shared some good hardy laughs with them about how he and the others had cajoled the hostile bandits into telling them about how to defeat them. He left them in good spirits with an understanding that he would return soon and continue their allegiance to Batu. Without hesitating, they assured him that they would follow orders just as he expected them to.

Hot running water, soap, and good, clean smells filled his home. He dressed and prepared to go out to get some good, hearty, healthy food. He was moving through the village trying to determine where he would eat when he spotted her. You couldn't help but notice her; she was captivatingly beautiful. Her familiar small gait was well known to him.

"Hello there Devine. It's been a while since I've seen you moving about. How've you been?"

"Zadok! My goodness, you are a sight for sore eyes. It's great to see you."

"Are your eyes sore?" he said with a slight smile.

"No! It's just a figure of speech. You look good. What have you been up to?"

"Marching, climbing, looking, rescuing; same old thing as usual. However, it's nice to see you though. I've just come off of an assignment and went home to shower and shave and clean up a bit and now I'm off to get some good hearty food; and a lot of it."

"You clean up quite nicely sir. How would you like to have dinner with my family? My mother always cooks enough for an army."

"That's a nice offer, but I wouldn't think of inconveniencing your mother."

"Don't be silly. You're hungry, and we have plenty of good wholesome home cooked food. Please. I'll be really offended if you turn down my invitation."

"Oh! We can't have that. Thanks for the invite. I'll follow you. Can I carry those bags for you?"

She handed over her packages and walked just a bit in front of him to the threshold of her front door. She opened it and ushered him into the foyer. "Please have a seat here, and I'll return in one moment. I just want to tell my mother that we have an esteemed gentleman with us this evening for dinner."

As instructed, he sat down and began to look around the house. He was quite impressed with the colors, plants, and décor. It was not plush or ostentatious; rather it reminded him of the simple elegance of the family. Everything smelled delicious, clean and fresh and welcoming. And whatever was going on in the kitchen filled the air with an aroma that was to die for. He was starving for some warm, well-seasoned good eats. He thought he detected the scent of fresh bread wafting in the air.

"Zadok! My friend, how are you?" said Vorce. "Welcome to my home. Devine tells me that you've just come off of an assignment and she found you wandering in the village trying to decide where to eat when you stumbled upon each other. I'm delighted to have you as our guest."

"Thank you ever so much. She was right. I was trying to decide just where to eat, and it seems God favored me with just the right place."

"Follow me to the table they're just about ready to serve."

They entered the dining room, and there he found the most sumptuous dishes lining the whole table. He was right he had smelled fresh bread baking; and there it was all soft, moist, buttery and hot. He could hardly stand it and felt like he could just thrust his face into all the platters at one time; he constrained himself and sat down. They waited momentarily until Devine and her mother Jasmine entered with their hands filled with luscious bowls of hot, steamy, rich foods. He caught himself swallowing and was careful not to drool and reveal his hungry state of being.

"Zadok. Thank you for gracing us with your presence for dinner. We are delighted to have you dine with us. We'll be ready in just moments. Please remain seated; we'll be right back."

Jasmine was as lovely as her daughter. He could immediately see where Devine got her good looks and demure stature. She had a bit of gray hair peeking out from beneath her shawl that he thought was unusual for her youthful face and figure. She was extremely graceful and genuine, and he instantly felt at ease. *"Please hurry up and bring out that food before I make a total and utter fool of myself. I'm starving, and I can hardly wait to taste those delicious dishes."* Jasmine, Devine and two of her siblings came out of the kitchen shortly thereafter. Vorce gave thanks for the food and began to pass each dish around the table for all to partake.

"Zadok, we are not used to having a guest of your strength and stature with us, please feel free to eat until your heart's delight. Both, Devine and my wife, fully enjoy cooking and they love to see others partake of their skills in the kitchen."

True to form, he ate until his heart was content. He tasted every dish on the table and was not disappointed. They marveled at his appetite, and they were totally delighted to see him comfortable enough to dine sufficiently. Finally, he sat back totally satiated and well pleased.

"I cannot thank you enough for such a wonderful meal. Having been on an assignment away from home, I was not eating wholesomely. That made this meal extra special. Many thanks."

"It was totally our pleasure to have you as our guest. Please know that you are always welcome at any time. Won't you join us in the garden for tea or something cool to drink?"

"Tea will be fine, and I'd be delighted to join you all."

Vorce and Jasmine moved to the garden with Zadok and Devine trailing closely behind. He noticed that the other family members did not join them.

"Wow! This is so beautiful! Who's the gardener? Who has the green thumb?"

"Oh! That would be Devine. She loves gardening and plants and cultivating green and growing things."

He turned to Devine and said. "Hidden talents? You should be displaying your skills to everyone. Ever consider having your own business? These plants are gorgeous, and the baskets you have created are exquisite." Devine blushed slightly and said," Do you think so? Do you really like them?"

"But of course! I get around a lot, and I really believe that you could easily find a market for your natural talent."

"It's something to think about. If you ever find an area that you think is good, please let me know."

"I'll do that. I have fully enjoyed the evening, but I must rush off since I have to get up early for a meeting. Thank you so much for rescuing me from certain starvation."

He turned to her parents to thank them for the meal and hospitality. He mentioned to them that he had an important meeting in the morning and had to leave. He was invited to take something home with him, but he refused stating that he would be leaving on assignment again soon and would not have the time to enjoy it. Vorce escorted him to the door. They shook hands and Zadok left wishing that he could have taken Devine with him.

Never late, Zadok joined the others for an early morning meeting to rehearse their plans. In a day or so he and his men were expected to rejoin the bandit gang and learn more about the timing of the plan to attack Jubilee. It would probably be his last visit home for a while. After the meeting, he decided to take a walk over by the bluffs to think things over, make a few decisions and clear his head. He had a lot of weight and responsibility and many things to consider.

"Now you know better than to be up this early and out here by yourself without an escort. Does your father know you are out here?" asked Zadok.

Deep in thought, Devine was startled just for a moment. "No, he does not! And for your information, I come out here to be alone and to think, pray and talk to God. I love this spot; it's so beautiful especially as the sun comes up over the mountains. It paints the whole sky with soft orange and melon colors with strips of baby blue peeking here and there. It's simply breathtaking."

"I can't argue with you on that point. It happens to be one of my favorite places on the island also. What could possibly be of such concern for someone as young and lovely as you?"

"Zadok you really have to stop saying that I'm so young, Years have passed since I was introduced to the community. I'm a full-grown woman, capable of thinking and deciding things all on my own. Just because you're a few years older than me doesn't mean that I am not mature."

"Whoa there! I apologize if I made it seem like you were not a woman or mature enough to make decisions. That is certainly not what I think. I did not mean to upset you."

"I'm not upset. I just wish you would stop treating me as though I am a child. It's infuriating that you can't see that I am a woman, not the little girl you're used to protecting."

"Oh! Make no mistake about it Devine, I know all too well that you are a woman."

"You don't act like it. You always stand about ten feet away from me. You're always at full attention whenever you do speak to me. You rarely make eye contact with me and when you do you retreat into this father-like posture that I really do not understand since you know my father quite well."

"Hmm. Have I offended you? I was only trying to be respectful as you deserve."

She held her hand up. "Never mind. I have said too much already. You're right I should go home. We enjoyed having you for dinner last night." Quickly she stepped to the left, turned around and proceeded to exit the area. Before she could take a full step, he positioned himself in front of her blocking her exit. "Devine, obviously I have sent the wrong message. I am so very sorry to have frustrated you today."

"Don't worry about it. I hope you'll be safe on your assignment." She began walking away, but before she was out of earshot he said, "Devine I have to leave on assignment in a day or so, but before I leave, I'd like to know if you would consider having lunch with me in the square?"

She stopped and turned to face him. "Just the two of us?"

"Yes. If your father will give his permission and of course if you wouldn't mind the company."

She could smile the biggest smile when she wanted to. She could signal that she was happy without uttering a word. "I'd love to have lunch with you tomorrow if you can make it."

"I can make it. Will you have someone escort you to the square or should I present myself at your home?"

"Come to the house about noon time if that is good for you."

"It's perfect. Will you allow me to see you home? It's still quite early?"

"Only if you will walk next to me and not behind as though you are guarding me against something."

"I can do that."

Twelve o'clock sharp he was at the door to call on Devine. Vorce met him at the door, welcomed him in and announced that his oldest son would accompany them to the square as was appropriate. Zadok nodded with full understanding and engaged Vorce in conversation until Devine appeared. She was ravishingly dressed in an array of earth tone colors that fully complemented her complexion. Nothing could adequately hide the shine in her eyes which were large almond-shaped discs of warmth and joy. He escorted her to his military vehicle which was whistle clean. He explained to her that it was always essential that it be close by for his use; she nodded that she understood. With her brother in full tow, the three of them drove to the square, parked and entered a popular restaurant for lunch.

After being shown a table, her brother excused himself to speak to some friends who were close by. He shook Zadok's hand and bent and kissed his sister on the cheek. She looked at him lovingly as he scurried over to the table with his friends.

"Can you recommend anything in particular?" he asked.

"I've been here many times. It's one of my favorite places to eat out. Everything here is good. It depends on what you want to eat. Do you want meat? If so, what kind?"

"Meat; definitely meat. Chicken preferably. Any suggestions?"

She reviewed the menu with him and ordered for both of them without hesitating. He was delighted with her choices and the ease with which she took control. He towered over her at the table, but she managed to level the playing field with her light-hearted jokes and easy style of conversation. He was totally relaxed.

"When are you leaving on your assignment?"

"Tomorrow. I'll be gone for a couple of weeks at a minimum."

She was silent, and he noticed a slight look of disappointment in her eyes. It impressed him.

"I am so happy to have spent a moment or two with you before I leave. I fully enjoyed the meal and the company."

She looked directly at him and was silent. He had no idea what to say next; there was an awkward silence, and they finished their drinks.

"Devine, what is that I am doing to upset you? Just a moment ago you were laughing and seemed to enjoy the meal, and now I 've said or done something to disturb you again."

"It is not what you have done. Rather, it is what you are not doing that is distressing."

He felt like an ant; a teeny-weeny little ant next to her. She had totally unnerved him, and he had no idea what to do about it.

"Zadok, may I ask your advice and counsel on a personal matter?"

"Certainly. I will answer it honestly if I can."

"I have a very dear friend who is actually quite fond of one of the men under your command. He seems to like her, and she is especially drawn to him. They have spoken casually and known each other for years. He is quite often on guard or away on assignments, and so they don't have a chance to really engage in any meaningful conversation. Plus, to make matters worse, he is very formal, very disciplined in a true military sort of way. You know that in our society young ladies do not approach men but must wait on them to seek her out. There never seems to be an opportune time for this to occur because of his responsibilities. Can you suggest something to make it easier for them to communicate?"

"Do I know this young lady?"

"I believe you do. "

"Perhaps, I could intercede and direct his attention to her. I could act as an intermediary and establish a time when he could possibly meet her in a casual environment. Maybe right here in the square. What do you think?"

"Do you think if he met with her and dined with her that he would be able to ascertain that she is waiting for him to approach her and seek permission to spend time with her?"

"Most of my guys are extremely sharp, very astute at reading behavior; it's part of the job."

Silence.

"And you are certain that he'll be able to ascertain the intent of the meeting?"

"Oh yeah! I'll make sure that he understands that she is fond of him so that he will know how to handle himself if he has any interest."

"Okay. Because you know respectable women can only go so far when they are interested in a man."

"Yes. I know that; it is as it should be."

Silence. He noticed that her eyes had darkened most recently, and it seemed as though a cloud was hovering over the table although the sun was blazing brightly. She adjusted her shawl and took a long look at him before indicating that she was ready to go. He paid the bill and looked around for her brother who was seated close by as before.

Zadok was a bit intimidated, but he was no fool, "Devine. I know that you are a good friend who is interested in assisting in this matter. However, I was wondering if you would consider allowing me to take permission from your father to spend time with you when I return? I have wasted a lot of time watching from afar as you have grown into a very resilient and strong young woman. I would be certain to hurry home if I knew there was any interest on your behalf in our spending time together."

Devine was young but very mature. She knew what she wanted, and she was spirited enough to go after it. She knew that she wanted to spend time with Zadok. She had always felt him watching over her even as a young child he was always near. She had watched him grow into a stalwart man capable of great leadership. He was always on point. Always ready to take action in any situation yet, here he was obviously uncomfortable with expressing his feelings. It was a curious situation for her.

"Zadok, if you had let this moment go without asking to spend time with me, I would have hunted you down in the middle of the night, totally masked and undercover and done great bodily harm to you. I know martial arts you know?"

She laughed out loud, and he joined her in a hearty chuckle. She was an amazing woman, and he was delighted with himself that he had moved beyond his fear of this five-foot five woman and spoken to her of his innermost desire to spend time with her. There was a pause of a moment or two when she spoke to him.

"Sir. I would be delighted to receive your company when you return home. And sir, I have waited a very long time for you to notice that I'm not a little girl anymore and that the woman in me is overjoyed that you have finally noticed that."

"I'm not the kind of man that easily can come up with lofty phrases to impress a woman. However, I have always noticed you, but because of my focus on my career, I pushed you out of my mind. I can no longer do that because my eyes are filled with your image, my mind is brimming with the way you walk and talk and the tilt of your head when you laugh. I know when you have been in the room. I know when you are disturbed. I know that you are a bit feisty and I like that about you. I know that I will hurry home with you in mind."

"Please exercise great caution. I will be waiting patiently for your safe return."

Shortly after, they all returned home. He waited a moment for Vorce to see him off. He thanked her father for giving him the opportunity to spend time with Devine and asked if when he returned, he could have permission to spend more time with her. Vorce touched him on the shoulder and assured him that he had his full permission to speak with Devine. Before he left the home, Vorce shook his hand heartily. "God speed my friend. This family will be praying for your safe return."

Chapter Thirty-Seven

Zar and Bosher called the island elders together to advise them that they were both getting married. They were met with a warm congratulatory reception from them. Once they reported that they planned on getting married within a very short time of each other the place was filled with cheers, handshakes, slaps on the back, and hugs and encouragement of every manner and sort. Once the information had been given, they asked for guidance on how to proceed with the marriage ceremony since neither of them had ever been to the wedding of a High Priest or Head Elder before. The older more seasoned elders assisted them with recommendations for the big days ahead. It was decided that Zar and Sierra would marry first and then be followed by the marriage of Bosher and Libi as a mere matter of respect. Plus, both Zar and Bosher wanted to be the presiding priest for their separate weddings: Zar would preside over Bosher's wedding, and in kind, Bosher would preside over Zar's wedding.

Zar returned home and spent time speaking with the family about timing. Everyone agreed that the wedding would be in thirty days. Sierra and Zar had already been betrothed to each other; the house on Mount Mizaan and the acceptance of Allure reflected the sanctity of the marital relationship. Sierra belonged to Zar as his wife, and she would have no other man. The plans were in place and the invitations set for release. Zar pulled Sierra aside for a quick moment. "Are you okay with the date being so soon? If not, I can delay the ceremony until you are comfortable?"

"I'm fine and just a bit anxious to be your wife. I am eager to proceed. I know exactly what I want to wear and who I want to be close to me during the ceremony."

"Okay. I just wanted to make certain the timing was fine with you."

"It is. I'm excited."

They joined the rest of the family and continued with the wedding plans. Invitations were prepared for a host of people from Jubilee and the mainland. Family and friends from both sides would fill the area and festivities would certainly be entertained for many hours. Bosher was prepared to officiate over the ceremony and totally cherished the honor. Food and delicacies were to be brought in from everywhere, and Monave planned to create a special cake that would be unimaginably beautiful as her gift. She also outlined a plan to fill more than twenty platters with special little sandwiches, tiny pies, and delicacies. Meats and fish of every sort were to be sautéed, fried, braised, grilled, roasted and smoked for the event. Vegetables and fruits would be delivered from numerous cultures and countries for the delight of everyone. No stone was left unturned for the wedding of the High Priest of Jubilee and his lady love and wife–Sierra.

It wasn't long before the big day arrived which was attended by everyone who was anyone on Jubilee and from many distant places. The Ketuba had been signed which was the marriage contract and Sierra had accepted the ring which she would wear during the ceremony.

The Chuppah canopy was huge to symbolize its importance. As planned, Bosher presided over the ceremony to the delight of everyone. Anyone who knew them was familiar with the close bond of brotherhood between Zar and Bosher. Sierra accepted the ring presented by Zar as she stood so elegantly adorned in white and gold. Her outfit was stunning, but her glow outshined the extraordinary fabric of the wedding outfit she wore. Her parents and friends were struck with the obvious joy that emanated from the couple as they joined in holy matrimony. The celebration was extreme as the whole community celebrated the couple's union. It was a true simcha moment–sheer ecstatic rapture and joy; spiritual rejoicing and exultation for the union.

For Zar, it was a Mitzvah moment when he, Sierra and God were joined as one. His heart swelled within him for he had waited so very long for this moment. His personal sacrifices in maintaining his moral decorum and keeping himself under control in the face of so many advances and opportunities to forsake his commitment to God and self–had paid off. Joy as no one could express filled his soul, and when he looked at his new bride, he knew that it was a shared expression of fulfillment.

The celebration seemed as though it would go on forever as the couple prepared to exit in a white carriage covered with flowers drawn by a white horse. The carriage carried them to the pier where they sailed away in a private boat to the other side of Mount Mizaan. Before exiting the vessel, they had changed their clothes into something comfortable and traveled via foot to the home he had especially built for her. They stood hand-in-hand at the crest of the hill overlooking their home. The scene was awe-inspiringly breathtaking. It seemed that God had swept His Hands over the outline and painted it with His special brand of love just for them. Everything seemed to sparkle, glisten and gleam from the paintbrush of the maker of the universe. They did not speak but walked slowly toward the house; breathing slowly, hearts beating rhythmically, emotions careening carefully together pitched at just the right meter.

Before they reached the threshold of the door, they glanced about and saw Allure and Koach in the door of the stables next to each other nodding as though each was affectionately rendering their approval. The ocean was the most beautiful lucid aqua blue imaginable; the sky was filled with pure white puffy clouds on a pallet of blues framed against the outline of lush mountains of indulgent greens, red and gold colors meshed together in harmony–beauty personified in an unforgettable memory. The splendid colors of the sky outlined against the mountains, and the lush forest greenery was mirrored in the water that sprawled before them. The only thing missing was a band of angels singing precious songs to celebrate their marriage. He opened the door for her and for the first time she had a full-blown picture of the home he had built for them. She knew without a doubt that he loved her. He thought of everything to express his total delight in marrying her. She could not improve on it at all–sheer perfection. She knew, as she had known before that God had answered her prayers –Zar was her blessing. Ever so slowly she turned and looked at her husband, their eyes met as he closed the door.

Chapter Thirty-Eight

The school at the west end of the island was just about fully completed. Bosher and Libi stood looking over it and discussing the final closing items. They were well pleased. In a few days, children from the mainland would fill the halls, classes, and dorms at the Center.

"I will leave in the morning to speak with Kila and Seth. I am certain they will be eager to join us here on the island."

"I wish I could be with you, but I am joining the militia on an important assignment and will be gone for a day or so. However, I do not want you to delay in getting them here. We have been away from then too long, and I am very concerned about Kila."

"I am too. I will leave early in the morning and return by late afternoon with them. We'll all be very eager for your return."

"Libi, will you tell them of our plans to marry very shortly? I think it would be best to let them know as soon as possible and to let them know that we plan to adopt them once we are married. Once I return, I will sit with them and affirm our decision."

"Yes. Is there something you are not telling me? Are you involved in something dangerous that I should be concerned about?"

"Nothing for you to be alarmed about; God has always taken good care of me, and I will be home in a few days."

As promised, she left in the morning at daybreak. She landed on the mainland and went straight to the school. She had discussed with the administrator's which children she would take with her so that their belongings were all prepped for departure. She sent for Seth and Kila to come into her old office. They were surprised and absolutely delighted to see her. Kila ran to her with open arms as soon as she spotted her.

"Still not ready to speak to me, little one? That's okay. You'll settle down soon and then I will have the pleasure of hearing your lovely voice. Seth; are you too old for a hug?"

"No Libi. I just did not want to run over Kila. It is so good to see you." He moved quickly to her side and hugged her affectionately.

"Children, Bosher and I have decided to take you both to the new school on Jubilee so that we can be closer to you. He is away on a mission right now, but he will join us in a few days. Is this acceptable to you both?"

Kila stood still; her eyes bright with affirmation. Seth looked her directly in her eyes and shook his head. It took him a moment to speak.

"You and Bosher have covered us and protected us like we have not known in years. We are so very grateful that you have decided to take both of us because we cannot be separated. I have no words to thank you with adequately, but please know that we will not be any trouble and will be certain to make you proud of your decision."

Libi smiled, "Seth you are so very mature for your age. However, Bosher and I want you to enjoy the rest of your youth; the youth that was stolen from you for so many years. Bosher has asked me to marry him, and once we are married, we intend, with your permission, to adopt both of you so that we can live as a family."

Tears streamed down Kila's face, she trembled with joy and she ran to Libi, who was sitting down, moved her hand and climbed into her lap. Immediately, Libi cuddled her and began to stroke her hair. "It's okay baby. You're safe now. We will be a family soon, and we have pledged not to let any harm come to you again. You will smile, you will laugh, and you will speak again."

Seth totally melted and moved to wrap his arms around her neck. He didn't speak, but she knew what he was thinking and feeling. They were silent for a moment, enjoying the fellowship of family.

"Okay. Go to your rooms and gather your things together. I have a few details to attend to before we leave. There are thirty other children going with us also. We'll meet in one hour in the lobby. Any questions?"

Just like true children, they shook their heads in tandem and ran off to their rooms. Libi left to set up the arrangements for travel for all of them and then returned to the lobby to usher the whole band of them off to Jubilee and their new homes. The trip was uneventful enough. Paperwork from Zar had already been forwarded to Pruvia for their admission, so they went through without a hitch. Seven guards met them on Pruvia and escorted them to the west end of the island and their new school. Once there, the children were met by a counselor who welcomed them into their new home and gave them a full tour of the facilities. After the tour, each child was assigned a room and then told to meet in the dining room for lunch.

"Wow! This place is beautiful. You put a lot of work into this. Thank you."

"Seth, we are fully committed to all of the children who have been hurt, harmed or maimed in any way. With God's blessing, we will make a positive contribution to their lives. Do you like your rooms? It is only temporary until after we get married and then you will both come to live with us and attend the school during the day."

"It is more than we could ever have asked for. Things are perfect, and we cannot wait to be a family with you and Bosher. Have you heard from him? Is he okay?"

"I'm sure that he is, and he'll join us in a day or so."

The transition went smoothly. All of the children seemed to adjust quite well to their new domain. Counselors and the medical team were introduced to them readily as were the teaching staffs of the new school. A full assessment was completed on each child, and their schedules were laid out for them to follow.

His assignment went well and as soon as he could he left for the school, Libi, Seth and Kila. He entered the garden and the gates when she saw him.

"Bosher! Bosher! Baba! Father! you came back for me just as you promised." Kila sprinted towards him and wrapped her arms around his legs.

He could scarce believe it. She spoke; she uttered his name. It totally threw him off guard; without thinking, he scooped her up in his arms and held her tightly. "Kila, Kila you are speaking. Kila, I have waited so long to hear your voice again. I have prayed and prayed and prayed for God to help you to relax and feel safe again, and He did it. Thank you, Father!" He twirled around and around with her in his arms, laughing, praying and singing her name over and over again.

Libi stood in the doorway witnessing the pure unadulterated love of a man with his daughter. Nothing was more natural; nothing was more satisfying than to see the two of them bonding and affirming their love for each other. She had never heard Kila speak before and it was music to her ears. Overcome with emotion she moved slowly towards them and waited for them to re-enter the earth for they had surely been on a spiritual journey together. When he saw her, they both opened their arms, and she joined in their blissful moment. Peace overcame them, and they stood there together fully breathing it in.

"Where is Seth?" Bosher asked.

"I sent for him to join us in the garden. He should be here any moment."

"I heard her. I heard her speak your name. I heard Kila utter words again. It means she is happy and comfortable and feels safe again." Seth looked at his sister with tears glistening in his eyes and walked over to her decidedly and touched her face. He had longed to hear laugh again, longed to hear the lilt in her voice or the sweet sound of music when she was singing. He kissed her on the forehead, took her hands and uttered her name.

"Kila. Kila. I am so happy that you are able to speak again."

"Brother. Seth, you have always been near to me, always been protective of me. I was just so afraid of what horrible thing might happen next that I could not breathe words although I wanted to. And now, we are going to be a family with Bosher and Libi. I feel safe knowing that you will be with me."

Seth turned to Bosher and said," You have been more than a friend to us, more than a priest to us, more than an overseer for us, from the beginning you were making your way into our hearts as a father. I hope to make you proud of me as a son."

Before he could speak, Kila turned to Bosher and said," Is it true? Is it really true? Are you going to marry us?" He laughed at the childlike way she spoke to him.

"Yes dear. I am going to marry all of you. I am willing and eager to marry all of you very soon." Turning to Seth, he said, "Seth, I cannot think of a young man that I would want to be a father to and to claim as my son, other than you. You are some kind of young man, and I am extremely excited to claim you as my own; I am very proud of you."

Bosher looked up in search for a connection with Libi's eyes. He saw the affirmation he sought, and although he wanted to take her into his arms, he restrained himself. There would be plenty of time for that in the near future.

"I have an announcement for all of you," he bellowed. I found a house; that is very near here that with a bit of work, a tweak here and there, I think will be perfect for us. Care to take a ride with me?" The children ran outside to get into the car.

"I'm so glad that you are back. I've made some strides on the wedding plans that I need to discuss with you. I missed you. Are you here for a while?"

"Are we getting married tomorrow? The next day? Yes. I am here for a while unless something unexpected happens. I plan to spend time getting the house ready for all of us so that we can move in immediately after the wedding. Can we have dinner tonight to discuss the plans?"

"Yes. Let's go to see the house you've found which I am certain will be perfect."

"It absolutely must be because it is for you. It needs some additions, but I have the team lined up and ready to go as soon as we agree on what we want. Let's go join the children."

Indeed, the house needed some work. However, it sat on a perfect lot of land. The scenery was breathtaking. The house was small. Perhaps it had been a cabin for someone at one time. The foundation was secure and would easily accommodate the new additions. They walked around the land and discussed where and what to add to the house. Once he had a good idea of her dream, he knew exactly what to do. The landscape alone made you want to reside there. Mountains loomed in the distance; it had a lake that reflected life brimming with fish, fields for grazing animals and it was large enough for a bountiful garden. It was perfect. He would enlarge the kitchen, add four bedrooms, a dining room, a front foyer, pantry, and enclosed garden area. He planned a complete back yard that children would adore that would be adjacent to a herbal garden for Libi to partake of. If he got started immediately, it wouldn't take long to complete with the team he had standing by.

They returned to the school so that the children could prepare for dinner, a bath and a restful night's sleep. Libi told them that she would see them both in the morning and Bosher assured them that he would be working hard and fast to complete their home. Before he left, he told Kila that he had not forgotten that she wanted her room to be pink. She smiled, hugged and kissed him and said, "I love you. Thanks for being my father."

He hugged Seth and affirmed his commitment to check on them intermittently while working on the house.

"Seth, would you like to help us work on the house when we get the framing done?"

"Oh yes! I would love that. I know how to work with tools, and I learn quickly."

"Okay, son. It's a deal. We can do it together."

He and Libi had dinner that evening and reminisced about the day. He listened while she told him about the plans for the wedding. He fully agreed with her plans and thought that it fit their style perfectly. She planned for it to take place in six weeks; he was overjoyed. It would give him ample time to complete the house and get everything ready for his family.

Chapter Thirty-Nine

Zadok and his men left early in the morning under disguise. He joined the marauder band and quickly got an understanding of his assignment on Jubilee. It would be a little while longer before the bandits would be ready to return to Jubilee with supplies. They advised that the full out strike to Jubilee would probably be in about six months. He learned that in the meantime, they planned to raid a nearby village; take women to sell as slaves for sexual favors, men as slaves to the highest bidders and the children to sell for various reasons. The village was small and poor and not apt to put up a distinct fight. However, they knew that there were several strong young men that lived there, so they had to plan for any and every possibility. The captain of the band's name was Deg. He planned to send out a reconnaissance team to scout out their options. Zadok reported that he had participated in many such events and would like to go along to see if he could add anything to the scheme. Deg liked his initiative and agreed to let him scout with the team. They left the next night on the nefarious mission.

Zadok went out with a team of about four men. They determined to scout out the area on various sides for possible avenues of escape and to shut them down effectively. It took them about two days to obtain sufficient intel about the strike to report to Deg. While he was gone, he assigned one of his men to steal away and get a message to Batu about the strike on the village in order to try to thwart the advance on the village. Once Zadok returned from the recon mission he participated in rendering the report to Deg.

Additionally, he assisted in planning a strategy that was certain to render them the slave bounty they desired. They decided to wait for the next full moon in order to have adequate light to effectuate their plan. Zadok left to join with his men and was assured that the message had been sent to Batu with approximate timing.

At the next full moon, Deg and his men along with Zadok and his team planned on leaving for the village. As planned, they circled the village blocking off all areas of escape. The plan was to steal into the tents, as they had done so many times before; and frighten the startled villagers into giving up without a fight. They formed teams and spaced themselves in various areas just outside the tents. Quietly, ever so quietly, they removed their knives and slit holes in the tents big enough for them to enter. As they did so, they bent down and removed the blankets from the people only to find bags of burlap filled with seed. No one was there; the whole village was totally empty although there was a full-fledged bonfire burning in the center of the village. Discovering this event, Deg became alarmed when he heard noises moving through the thrushes in the woods. He heard dogs barking and the sound of knives and sickles making their way toward the village. He became apprehensive and knew instantly that somehow the villagers had become alerted to the attack and were now moving in on them. He called for his men to retreat since it sounded like there were many more of them.

Quickly Deg marshalled his men together so that they could escape effortlessly through the woods via the route that they entered. It sounded like there were hundreds of them; he could not understand how his plans had been thwarted. There was no evidence that the village had so many men. Perhaps they had discovered that they were being scanned for attack and solicited support from other local villages. Zadok quickly took charge and lead the retreat through the woods and back to the campsite. Once there he was furious with Deg.

"Look! If this is the way you plan an attack, I don't think we want to support you anymore. We almost lost our lives. Are you telling me that the last recon we did was the first time you had any surveillance done in the village?"

"Hey! I was just as surprised as you were. I have no idea where all of those men came from."

"That's my point exactly. When you have an operation this big, you do a couple of sourcing missions to get the lay of the land. See how the people live and move about. You can't find that out in one trip."

"Okay, okay. We got out of there in one piece thanks to your quick thinking. Whew! That was a close one."

"Yeah, but I don't like close calls. I like to take care of business so that I minimize any trauma to myself or to my men. I hope you have a better plan than that for attacking Jubilee."

"Well, for my part we are good, and I am not in charge of the attack on Jubilee. My team is support."

"Um hum. Do you know anything about the head guy planning the attack? Are you certain he knows what he is doing?"

"Yes. We met with him years ago when he was working with a paramilitary organization. That group was a combative force that was exceptional. He was extremely good and rose to the level of a Nagad. Plus, he has an inside straight since he started as one of them at the School of the Prophets. We're good. This guy is a master of deception and warfare. I am very comfortable with him leading the advance. His plan is foolproof and will benefit all who participate. Relax. I'm sorry about tonight, but you can be certain that will not happen again."

Zadok turned away to join the troops he was aligned with. He talked to them quietly and affirmed that Batu had been able to change the whole outcome of the attack by Deg and his team of marauders. He complimented them on their performance and encouraged them with the fact that he was learning more and more about the planned attack on Jubilee. They were performing an important part of protecting their family and friends on Jubilee. As soon as he could, he sent a report to Batu about what he had learned about the attack and that in fact, it was Natas who was leading the planned attack on Jubilee.

Batu received the message and smiled knowing how easy it was to thwart the advance on the village. Not one man, woman or child had been injured. He and a small troop of men had gone to the village and advised the village chief of the plan. Together they gathered the women and children and sent them to a nearby friendly village that was significantly larger for safety. Then the village men and the troops with Batu filled bags with grain and seed and covered them over making it look like they were all asleep. At exactly the right time they took dogs, large knives and sickles and began making noise as though cutting through the brush to rush the men in the camp. They made a lot of noise using the men in the village, those from the larger friendly village and Batu's men to sound like they were advancing on Deg's team to storm them and engage in a fight that surely Deg could not win because he was outmanned. Thus, Deg and his men raced off into the woods in full retreat.

Later, Batu convinced the village chief to partner with the larger friendly village elders so that they could merge resources which would benefit each of them. Immediately after, he returned to

Jubilee with his troops and a bag full of laughs and chuckles on how they made the big bad Deg team of marauders scamper off like whipped dogs.

Chapter

Forty

All of a sudden Havi popped his head up out of a dead sleep. Moments ago, he was dreaming the best of dreams when he became aware that something was awry; he sensed that something was different– lounging one moment and the next on alert. He shook himself awake, stretched and peered around. Things were quiet, things were calm, but he decided he better look around just to be certain that all was well. He rounded the corner and stopped short taking in all of the activity. That's when he saw them easing into the shop. Ever so carefully they entered the front door and were on their way to the back of the store. He kept quiet so he could assess their intent–he laid low and moved about in stealth mode just waiting.

Her hands were full of fabrics and crafts, soaps and oils as she turned the corner to place them on the counter. Doing so, she did not see them until she turned around to retrieve more products.

"Oh, my goodness! You startled the life out of me! Jez! When did you get in? I'm so glad to see you. You must be very good at what you do because I did not hear the door alarm sound at all. Is it broken?"

"No! I temporarily disengaged it so I could surprise you; I'll fix it right now. But the surprise worked. Remember when I told you to keep your head up and your eyes open?

"Yes, but who knew you would go sneaking around as though you were on a special assignment in the marshes somewhere."

"I am on special assignment, and my special assignment is you." A big wide smile filled the whole expanse of his face.

"Jet, how nice to see you just wait until Havi finds out that you're here. Havi! Havi! Come here."

Jet looked around for him and was surprised when his little friend did not respond. His ears went up, and his tail was standing straight out–he was curious about what could have happened to him. They all were looking around when Havi burst from under the tablecloth and pounced on Jet's front paws with all his weight. All of him soaking wet was no disturbance to Jet as he looked down at the small black ball of fur. He took his nose and poked him gently, and Havi rolled over as though mere dust. Monave and Jezreel roared with laughter at the two of them and how they teased each other. After he nudged him Jet's tail began to wag, and his eyes gleamed to see his little friend again.

"Gosh, it's so nice to see you. How long are you here for?"

"Not long. My assignment is quickly advancing, but I wanted to speak with you so…"

"I'm so glad to see you. Can you come home and have dinner with us and then you and I can talk alone in the garden?"

"Yes, of course. I'll go home and clean up and be there for dinner. Can I go and return to walk you home?"

" I have to drop off an order for someone, so I'll meet you at the house at 6:00. Okay?"

"I'll be there. Jet, come on. I've never seen you so playful until you get around Havi."

Six o'clock dragged by slowly but finally, he found himself at the front door. He was welcomed in and ushered out to the garden to talk with Vorce and the family while Monave and her mother prepared the meal. As expected, it was exceptional, warm and filling. Afterward, he and Monave sat in the garden area and talked about all manner of things. They got along so famously having many of the same interests and concerns. They laughed about old times, people, and stories of assignments and naturally, they laughed about the time he totally frightened the two unruly sailors in the shop. As the evening began winding to an end, he turned to her slowly and said, "Mo, will you consider being my wife? I promise I will never leave you or deceive you. I will never allow anything or anyone to hurt or harm you. I will try to be all that you could want in a husband and a friend. I have waited so long to approach you and get the nerve to ask you to be my very own wife."

There was a moment of silence before she answered, "Of course. I cannot imagine being with anyone else. You are most certainly all that I need and want. When you return from your assignment, we can speak to my father about a wedding."

"Actually, I wanted to do that tonight. I have a ring that I purchased some time ago with me. He pulled it from his pocket, "Do you like it?"

Surprised and curious she untied the ribbon quickly and opened the box to find the most perfect ring ever designed. There sat the most brilliant diamond she had ever seen surrounded by delicate opals and rubies which reflected their shine in the face of the diamond. It was spectacular. Tears welled up in her eyes, her breathing became halting, and her palms were wet with perspiration. Her fingers covered her mouth as she gasped at the thought of it all. She opened her mouth to speak to him as she looked up, but no sound came out. A slow yet steady stream of tears flooded her face. He reached up to wipe them away.

"Prayerfully these are tears of joy for I will do all in my total ability never to have a tear touch your face again. I cannot express my delight in knowing that you have accepted me."

"Jez, I am overcome with emotion. Yes, I am more than willing to be your wife."

"Mo, I also have been left a good deal of land that I inherited from my father. When I return, you can choose the site that you would like to live on and then we can lay plans for our home. I am far from rich, but I do have the means to take care of you quite comfortably."

"I have no concerns about your caring for me. You are such an honorable man, so traditional in your demeanor that I am not concerned at all. Before you leave, please allow me to gather my family so they can be included in our plans."

He nodded, and she moved to collect them all. Jaya and Vorce appeared together in the room and welcomed him with open arms. Cherish, and the boys joined them shortly thereafter, and the family was expanded and knit together in that very moment. They prayed together before he left and sought God for his safe return.

Chapter

Forty-One

Six weeks expired so quickly, but Bosher had managed to finish the house to the exact specifications of Libi's design. He kept his word and made certain that Seth had work to do to contribute to the design and building of the house. It was a true bonding moment in time for them. The house was idyllic just as they had planned; simple, elegant, pristine, quiet and peaceful. The wedding was scheduled to happen in two days. Bosher had one last element to add. Something he thought that she would cherish as a special gift to her. He called Mingo to determine if it was finished and found that it was ready for delivery. He scheduled it for early the next morning–one day before the wedding.

Friends and family from everywhere joined them for the celebration. The whole community of Jubilee honored him much as was done for Zar's wedding. And of course, Zar presided over the ceremony making it ever so much more special. Best friends to the end; brothers who were inextricably joined in spirit as though flesh. They loved each other in the most wholesome manner possible; priests in total unison with each other as they reverenced God. Their wives were as sisters; the foursome cherished each other individually and collectively.

Libi insisted on making the Chuppah by hand. She engaged the most beautiful fabric she could find with the assistance of Monave's guidance. Creating the chuppah was her charitable act; her gift to the marriage that would become a family heirloom. She knew that the chuppah was a symbol of God's presence at the wedding and in the home of the couple. Thus, she took her time with every stitch. She prayed and envisioned each addition to the sacred cloth over which God would hover. The finished product was spectacular! They elected to have four of the priests to hold the chuppah poles which represented the community that would support them in their marriage. Marriage, the union of two people in a spiritual bond learning how to walk as one unit, was in full force during the wedding nuptials of Bosher and Libi.

Zar officiated over the whole ceremony reciting the Sheva Brachot, the seven wedding blessings over the marriage. Zar recited the Sheva Brachot which is a mosaic of interwoven Biblical words, phrases, and ideas with such depth and feeling that the audience scarcely breathed. Some of the words reflected both Grace to accept what one cannot change and recognition that everyone has unique and irreplaceable talents as keys to a harmonious marriage. He ended the seven blessings by saying," Blessed are You, LORD, our God, sovereign of the universe, who created joy and gladness, groom and bride, mirth, song, delight and rejoicing, love and harmony and peace and companionship. Quickly, LORD our God, there should be heard in the city of Jubilee and in the courtyards of the Temple the voice of joy and the voice of gladness, the voice of groom and the voice of bride, the jubilant voices of grooms from the bridal canopy and of young people from the feast of their singing. Blessed are You, LORD, Gladdener of the groom with his bride."

Food and music, music and food, song and dance-joy spilled over the whole community engulfing the newlywed couple. Seth and Kila danced around as though lifted on invisible puffs of air. Their little faces covered in total glee; freedom from fear; love and peace filled their hearts. A family had been born and joined together on the same day as the wedding. Spiritually bonded together in the wedding ceremony was the union of two children who had willingly been grafted into the lives of the new couple.

When the couple took their leave of the ceremony, they entrusted Kila and Seth to Zar and Sierra. They decided to go to their new home to change into more comfortable clothes before leaving for their special time together. As they stepped from the transport, he turned to her and asked her to cover her eyes. She did as requested, and he slowly guided her to the entrance of their new home. Once there, he gently removed her hands so that she stood directly in front of the special gift he had designed specifically for her. She gasped, leaned forward and slowly turned to him.

"No one has ever loved me like this. No one has ever peeked into my heart and mind and cared enough to express their love and concern for me like this. It is simply beautiful and captures all of my most precious thoughts."

"I asked Mingo to design it for me after giving him a bit of guidance. You cannot enter this home without getting a glimpse of the woman who resides within."

"I have no words to express my awe of it and how much I cherish the thought of it all."

She approached the statuesque fountain and lingered awhile just gazing at the carefully structured figure. Her eyes roamed over the four-foot figurine carefully. It was crafted from a natural stone that had been smoothed to perfection having a stream of water flowing from the curve beneath her arms. She was seated on a rock curled over with her arms folded around her knees with long hair gliding down her back. Children were nestled around her feet some standing, others sitting near her. Her arms appeared to gather them all close to her. The circumference of the fountain was filled with vegetation of all sorts and colors spilling onto the lush green of the lawn. It was as though she was sitting in a garden engulfed in the virtues of nature while embracing the children in a comforting manner. Soft lights lit the base of the statue where the water gathered and was recycled into a continuous flowing stream.

"You love everything and everyone. No one escapes your concern especially children, and in turn, they run to you in anticipation of your love for them. I have been blessed enough to have experienced the depth of your love and commitment to those you care about. I wanted to try to capture that in a fountain that welcomed others into our home. It does not do you justice, but it is a good try at a representation. Mingo did a good job; I am pleased."

"Thank you. Thank you for thinking of me in this way and for stretching to please me in this manner. I will cherish it and this moment forever. However, we better hurry if we are going to catch the ship. Aren't you excited?"

"Excited? I'm thrilled to be able to spend some much-needed time with you. Let's go."

Chapter Forty-Two

Night fell swiftly as they gathered themselves together to begin moving the necessary supplies into the caves on Jubilee. Deg had his men stationed at both entrances to the caves.

They lined up so as to make the movement easier as they passed the equipment to each other in pursuit of its final resting place in the caves. Their movement had not gone unnoticed. Batu and his men were stationed and on vigilant watch on both Mount Mizaan and the west end of the island. They knew exactly when Deg and his men had begun to move supplies, and they knew exactly what type of supplies were being gathered in the caves. Jezreel sent word to Batu of the mission but long before he had received the message Batu and his troops were aware of the stirring in the caves. After three days, Deg and his men completed their tasks and fell back onto the mainland to wait for further instructions from Natas.

In the meantime, Jezreel and his men had garnered enough information about the number of men Natas had gathered to attack Jubilee. The only thing that was uncertain was when they would strike. The plan of attack was well known to Jezreel and Bosher and they, in turn, shared every item with Batu and Zadok. All avenues of defense were aptly known and covered-there was no doubt that Jubilee was well protected from the onslaught. Further, they all knew that God was with them and that He alone would prevail. They all reasoned that when God was for you who could possibly stand against you? Each and every day they prayed for guidance and deliverance from the tempter and the deceiver of the people. No decision was made without seeking God's advice and council first; this guaranteed their success. They had no fear; they were anxious to get it over with so that they could get back to their wholesome lives.

Zar informed them that he was going to Mount Mizaan to speak with God. He had received a spiritual unction, a calling that he recognized as God telling him to "Come Up." He planned to leave first thing in the morning and would return as soon as possible. He assured them that nothing would happen until his return and that when he returned, they would have the Arm of God as a weapon. Nothing and no one could have been more prepared for an affront to Jubilee than the forces aligned by Batu, Jezreel, and Zadok.

Zar returned home to Sierra and informed her that he was leaving for the mountain in the morning because he had been summoned.

"Is everything alright? Will you be gone for a long time? Can I do anything to help you while you are away?"

"I promised that I would never lie to you and I will not begin to start now. Natas is planning to attack Jubilee so that he can take over the governance of the islands. There is nothing to be concerned about, we have known this for quite a while, and we have men stationed all over the island to notify us of any imminent threats."

She seemed shocked, and a bit startled never suspecting that anything of the kind was occurring all around her. However, she was not alarmed because she knew full well who Zar was and who he served. She knew that his trip to the mountain would benefit Jubilee since the people of God resided therein. And she knew that although he was the high priest of the islands that her husband was more than capable of leading and marshalling his forces against any foe.

"What shall I prepare for you to take? I love you, Zar. Do you need food or clothing or blankets? I am a bit anxious for you although I need not be. I'm very happy with you. Please be careful. I love you Zar, and I need you to return safely since I cannot raise this child by myself."

Swiftly he turned his head to look at his wife. He was certain that he heard her correctly.

"Sierra, are you saying that you are pregnant? How long have you known?"

"I was certain of it a few weeks ago, and I was waiting for the right time to tell you which I did not intend to do now it just slipped out perhaps because I wanted to give you a reason to come home and not take any unnecessary chances."

"You are more than enough reason to come home. Are you feeling okay? Shall I do something; get something for you before I leave?"

"Don't worry Zar. Keep your mind clear for the challenges ahead of you. I'll go home to mother until you return so you won't be concerned."

"Dearest, thank you so much for caring enough for me to carry my child. God is so good to us to bless us with a baby. I think it will be a boy and I want to name him Sierra Savion." He moved towards her and placed his hands upon her stomach. "Father, please bless this child and mother. Keep them safe and tucked beneath your mighty wings. Lord, God, thank you for a child with the woman I most dearly love."

"I am not naming my son Sierra Savion." She laughed in a good-hearted sort of way." We can deal with the name when you return home. We have quite a bit of time."

He took her to her mother's home and got her safely secured. Immediately thereafter, he left for the mountain and instructions on what and how to go about protecting Jubilee. Once he arrived, he toned down a bit and calmed his spirit. He breathed in and out slowly filling his lungs with pure fresh air. It took a few days of quiet meditation, praise, and worship for him to clear his mind and wait for the "Call." He ambled about just taking in the splendor of God's handiwork in nature. After about three days he was certain that he was to go to the crest of the mountain and prepare for his meeting. Given the circumstances on Jubilee, he knew that God would be actively involved and would clearly define how He wanted him to proceed. Once he arrived at the crest, he took off his shoes and waited. It was not long before the cloud descended. Nothing was quite like it; it never ceased to amaze him. It was truly undefinable, stupendous and glorious and beyond human imagination. He waited quietly until God spoke.

"You have been obedient, and I am proud of you. I know you wanted to engage Natas in battle, but you humbled yourself to My will. The reason I did not want you to fight him is that I wanted to give him every chance to repent, to change his mind and his ways but he has refused My spirit. He knows the way, he knows the truth and the light to salvation, but he refuses to succumb to My will. He is filled with the spirit of his father Satan; truly he bears the fruit of the evil one which is why he has always hated you. But he has gone too far this time. I cannot allow him to advance upon My people; those who have carefully elected to follow me in all their ways. Enough!"

Zar stood quite careful not to speak; not to question.

"When you return to Jubilee take Koach and meet him on the beach on Pruvia. He is not allowed to place his foot on the shores of Jubilee or on this mountain. If he or any of his men should venture to touch this mountain, I will pierce them with fire through and through until not even a cinder will be discovered. I will do the same if any of them takes up arms to challenge the peace that resides in Jubilee, but none of this will occur.

Take Koach, dress in your priestly uniform instead of that of war. You are to wear the Breast Plate, Epod, Robe, Sash and Turban with YHWH prominently displayed. Place a triangle shaped pure white flag draped in gold fringe with the crest of the temple on it over the head of Koach just in front of his chest. Let a golden tassel with three chords be placed at the midpoint. Assemble the armies of Jubilee around the parameter of Pruvia in plain sight. When the challenge begins, I will give you the words to speak to Natas.

Pray before you enter the battlefield because you will be tempted to resolve this matter in your own strength, but I admonish you not to do so. This battle is not yours; it is Mine and is as old as time itself. The battle of good and evil, divinity and deception, darkness and light are forever in conflict; but take heart My son it will not always be as such. I require that you pray and purge your soul from evil resentment. My wish is that there be not the slightest trace of resentment even suppressed in your heart when you meet with tyranny and injustice. Pray that he will humble himself before he is destroyed. Today, I will arise and fight the battle in a way that not one drop of blood will be shed which is not the way Natas

has planned it. Have no fear the battle is already won, and Jubilee is safe as it will forever be."

Zar was perfectly erect listening to every word of direction. He asked not one question nor made one comment. He understood his assignment perfectly well and was at ease with it. Suddenly the cloud began to ascend, and Zar fell to the ground prostrate before his maker. Just before it vanished into the heavens, he heard His voice say,

"You are more than welcome son. It is a healthy baby boy who will be totally dedicated to serving me. See to it."

Chapter Forty-Three

Natas called his senior commanders to his office. "How many forces do we currently have?"

"I estimated in excess of one thousand men who are ready to support your plan to attack Jubilee."

"Phenomenal! Call them together and notify them that we will strike Jubilee three weeks from today. They are to meet right here on Pruvia where we will stage our most critical strike and in so doing end it all. They do not have even one-third of the forces that we have. The plan is to attack in two places. First, a surprise attack on the west end section of Jubilee with Deg and his men. They will rush to handle that onslaught leaving us to pursue and advance directly into Jubilee. There will be some residual forces left behind to cover Jubilee, but it will not be sufficient to overtake us."

"We are ready, willing and more than able to overtake them and seize control of the Temple and government."

"Okay. I will meet you here in three weeks for the event of the century. Men, it will be well worth your effort. Jubilee is rich in resources of all kinds, and the spoils will be distributed evenly for your commitment. Once we take over, then we will discuss the administration of offices and responsibilities. You will be well pleased. They will rue the day they did not let me into their plans to rule Jubilee. Now it's too late. They will all bow down to me."

Now they had it. The time for the strike was set. Three weeks from the day, Natas planned to attack Jubilee. Jezreel, Bosher, Batu, and Zadok were ready. They would leave the contingency of forces who were already on the west end there to deal with Deg and his men. The rest would surround the perimeter of Pruvia, as directed by Zar and wait for the signal to engage the enemy if it should come.

Batu returned to the west end and informed his men of the well thought out plan. Zadok and his men would assist Deg in finishing the assignment at the caves. Zadok suggested to Deg that he and his men station themselves on the base of Mount Mizaan as they had done previously to assure that no one had discovered them prior to their attack on the west end. Further, they would act as watchmen as the ships carried the military supplies around the coast of Jubilee, disguised as a cargo ship, and into Pruvia where the artillery would be unloaded for Natas. When they had completed delivering the artillery, they would return to the caves to wait for the signal to attack the west end.

Because of his foolish blunder on the mainland with the village attack, Deg had gained a lot of respect for Zadok and thought the suggestion from Zadok was sage advice. After the supplies had been delivered to Natas, Deg and his men returned to the caves. Zadok assured him that all was well and that the plan was still in good stead. He suggested that they close off the second entrance with boulders as it originally had been to make certain that nothing looked suspicious since they had already moved the supplies. Deg agreed and sent his men to cover the opening. After doing such, he and his men returned to the mainland for a few days of pillaging in the outlining villages before the attack. They would return in ample time to meet their strategic deadlines. Zadok and his men remained behind. They took some time to spend with friends and associates before having to return to defend the devious plan Natas expected to render.

Chapter Forty-Four

Jezreel and Zadok took full advantage of the time they had off and away from their assignments. Jez moved at lightning speed to go home, change into some decent clothes and show up at the shop. Zadok was a bit slower trying to think of the most appropriate ways to see Devine again. He finally decided to chuck all the rules and regulations and simply call to invite her to dinner, a walk or something.

Jez called Monave at the shop and asked if he could take her for a walk and then to dinner.

"Yes. I can close the shop early and meet you at the house at four o'clock. Is that okay?"

"Perfect. I was thinking we could take our furry little friends with us for a walk along the beach. What do you think?"

"I love it, and I know Havi will be overjoyed to see Jet again. They get along so well."

Precisely at four o'clock, he showed up at the house with Jet. Ardash happened to be home and greeted him warmly. "Welcome. It's good to see you, and obviously, this is the famous Jet; he's quite big and ominous. Mo advised me that you two would like to take a walk with the dogs along the beach. Sounds like a great idea. I'll get my hat and join you." Jez swallowed and nodded because he knew without her father's approval she could not go.

Ardash chuckled and said," I'm only teasing you. I feel quite comfortable with you two walking in broad daylight with the dogs. Plus, you have made your intentions well known that you intend to marry my eldest daughter. It is good for you to develop your communication skills with each other. Good communication and a good understanding are critical to the success of a good marriage. Go with my blessing and please plan to have dinner with the family when you return. We like having you around knowing that we won't have to clean up and put a lot of food away when you dine with us." He laughed out loud. "I'm just kidding with you. You'll have to get used to my odd sense of humor."

Jez smiled and relaxed just as Mo entered the room with Havi. Havi immediately went over to Jet and put his paw on Jet's front foot. Jet swished his tail back and forth but did not move his paw. They were ready to go and impatiently waited on Mo and Jez. Mo chirped up, "Let's go these guys are ready to romp." So, they took off walking toward the beach area. While there they engaged in a lot of conversation. They talked about children, where to live, their personal future plans, finances, family input, the dogs, whether to live in the country area or near the city and port area and when to actually marry. They decided on sooner rather than later, and they wanted a small very intimate celebration; just family and very close friends. They decided to speak with her parents during dinner that evening.

Zadok took another venue to Devine. He wanted to make a big splash since it was apparent that she felt that he had ignored her for so many years. He made some contacts which included Mo and a few others and had six dozen baskets of beautiful flowers and plants sent to her home. He also sent several other baskets which included scarves and skirts and wonderful, delightful scents from all over the world. Mo added some of her latest designs in jewelry and her special little sweets wrapped in a crimson paper that sparkled and made you not want to open the package because the wrapping was so unique. Once they arrived, he waited, watching from a secure location so that he could determine what was arriving and when. When everything had been delivered, he took a deep breath and knocked on the door. Her mother Jasmine opened the door, and with a look of surprise pulled him into the foyer and pressed her finger against her lips,

"Shhh. She doesn't know you're here and she is having the most wonderful time opening and cherishing all the gifts you sent. Let's just wait a moment. Stand right here." He obeyed and from a corner of the room fully enjoyed watching Devine's animated behavior as she took in all the treasures.

About fifteen minutes into the gift opening occasion her mother said, "You have another gift that has just arrived, but I need your help to get it in the door." Devine jumped up immediately and ran to the door. Not finding anything there she turned to ask her mother where it was and ran smack dab into Zadok. He was well dressed, smelling very nice and masculine and obviously enamored with Devine. "Do you like your gifts?"

She was totally stunned and for once unable to speak if but for just a moment. "Zadok, there's so much, so many gifts and it is not my birthday. What a lovely surprise. Thank you. Thank you. Thank you."

"Are the gifts appropriate for a grown woman? Are they suitable for a full-grown lady who is unique and very, very special to me?"

Devine smiled the biggest smile ever, "You've made your point sir!"

"Have I earned your permission to approach with yet another gift? I must warn you that it is a gift for a fully-grown woman. Can I approach?"

She nodded her affirmation. Then slowly, very slowly, Zadok-Captain of the Guard, turned and faced Devine; a fully-grown woman and asked her to be his wife. He followed the question by presenting her with the most beautiful ring that he could find that resembled her special type of beauty. Her mother stood quietly aside with her hand over her heart, rhythmically patting herself as she watched.

Without hesitating, Devine responded with a resounding. "Yes!!" He took her hand and led her to the couch, and they sat down together. Jasmine entered the room and bent to hug him.

She was so obviously pleased with her new son. She left to call Vorce and ask him to come home as early as possible, and she informed him that Zadok had in fact presented Devine with a spectacular ring to seal the contract of marriage.

The family joined together later in the evening to celebrate the newly engaged couple. Vorce pulled Zadok aside and congratulated him. He shook his hand, and they spoke briefly about the future for the two of them. He assured Zadok that he had the full support and backing of the whole family. He asked if he would be leaving again soon and was informed that he would be around for about another week perhaps ten days. Vorce asked that in that time if it would be acceptable to open his home to a wedding announcement for close family and friends and Zadok fully agreed to do whatever would make Devine happy. Filled with joy and excitement, Vorce and Jasmine began planning the announcement of the engagement of their daughter Devine to Zadok to go out to family and friends immediately. They scheduled a celebration dinner to take place at their home in ten days.

The dinner was an overwhelming success. Devine was radiant and Zadok so elegant in his military dress uniform. He and Devine invited their closest friends and relatives and announced that the wedding would take place in the very near future. Members of his troop, Zar and Sierra, Batu and Ashima, Mingo and many others joined in the joyous occasion. At the end of the evening Zadok, Devine and her parents sat together after everyone had left and the house had been placed back in order. Collectively they prayed together. Vorce asked God to totally cover the couple with His blessing of health, wealth, and many children. Hearing the last requested blessing for many children, Zadok looked at Devine and winked; in turn, she winked right back at him and smiled. They closed the prayer with thanks and gratitude to," God the maker and sustainer of all things. To Him who loves deeper and more than any human being can ever understand and who is willing to forgive us of all of our sins once we repent and turn to Him who is eager to forgive and welcome us back into His arms. Father, please expand their territory together for Your honor and glory and never take Your Hand from them."

After the prayer, Zadok bid everyone good night and left for his home. Walking through the streets of Jubilee that night he felt an overwhelming peace. He stood still for a moment and looked up at the heavens trying to take in the splendor of it all. He knew right then, with peace and joy filling his whole being, that God was very real; that He was awesome, mighty in all things, a force that no one could contend with if they were his enemy. And right then he knew that the battle that was before them would be accounted to God for the sake of His people living in Jubilee.

He stopped looking about, stood erect, pulled his shoulders up and straightened his back; then, in total awe of who it was, he served he saluted God. It was a salute that only a soldier could understand. It was filled with the snap of respect, recognition, and obeisance that is due to the ultimate leader. His eyes were bright and filled with tears as he brought his right arm up to the brim of his hat. The snap of his arm, as he saluted God, caused his whole body to sway just a bit. He relaxed, took in a deep breath and sensed the indwelling spirit of God fill his being. *"What a night! What a phenomenal and most memorable night"* He headed home and Zadok–Captain of the Guard– was humming some tune that no one but him would ever recognize.

Chapter Forty-Five

The plan was set and the time was right. Deg had delivered the supplies to Natas as expected; there was plenty of it. He returned to the cave at the west end of Jubilee and signaled Zadok and his men that they were back. Zadok seemed to be delighted and informed Deg that indeed no one seemed to have discovered the opening to the cave. He suggested that they close up the opening as tightly as possible leaving just enough room for them to escape in the morning. He advised that he and his troops had brought in a worthy feast for the men to indulge in to celebrate the battle that was to begin the very next morning. Deg loved the idea and left to enter the cave and begin the celebration. Zadok and his men brought in a huge basket of tiny sweet pies that smelled delightful. Deg's men delved into the sweet goodies immediately followed by gobbling down veggies, meats, and potatoes, roasts and drink. It was not long before they all began to feel the sleepiness associated with overeating and drinking. Deg leaned against Zadok with his drink in one hand and a thick turkey leg in the other. He slurred his words as he said," Here's to victory! Here's to the long-awaited payoff for all of our troubles. Thanks to you and your men we were able to fulfill our part of the bargain and tomorrow I will be more than happy to pay you all quite well." He stumbled a bit as he tried to sit down.

"Careful there captain you don't want to injure yourself before the big day." Zadok steadied him into a sitting position against one of the boulders.

When they were all soundly asleep, Zadok and his men slowly left the cave. The drugs that were slipped into the sweet goodies, veggies, and potatoes had done their job. The men slept soundly. A quiet sadness came over Zadok as he looked at them sleeping knowing that they would never awaken again. *"Sad. They all had a chance to live another type of life but chose that of evil and destruction to others. However, they're human beings, and I pity them. What a fate–to die in a cave. For what? God rest their tired pitiful little souls."*

He signaled for his men to exit the cave. After the last one was out and on the other side, they carefully placed each boulder back in place–a pyre built of stone for Deg and his band of marauders. Now, all they had to do was to wait for the morning to effectuate the other part of the plan.

Morning came right on schedule. Zadok sent word to Natas that all was well and that they were ready for the plan to go into effect at high noon. They would not speak again until after the battle had ended. At high noon, Deg and his men planned to enter the west end and threaten the livelihood of the inhabitants at that end of the island. Once threatened, militia forces from Jubilee would immediately respond to the threat and thereby diminish the forces available to fight the good fight against Natas and his army. As high noon approached, Natas began to assemble his men. He planned to wait until about one o'clock to actually head toward the battlefield so that Deg's part of the plan could forge ahead. Unbeknown to him, Deg and his men had already been lost and buried in a cave.

Zar was notified that there was a militia that was assembling on Pruvia. He picked up the phone and called Nastas. The phone rang three times before Natas answered.

"Hello. I was expecting your call."

"Really? What is happening down there? I've been informed that some type of army is forming on the beach."

"The type of army is one that is stellar, apt and able to overtake any force that may try to stop them, and they are under my command."

"Hmmm. And just what is the purpose of the army under your command?"

"I have waited long enough for you to come to your senses and make me a part of the priesthood of Jubilee. If you had done, so there would have been no need for bloodshed and the loss of life such as these islands have ever seen. I would have been able to advance to the position of High Priest in a fair manner but… now I'll just have to take over on my own terms."

"And just what to do you expect to gain for all of your deception and evil plotting?"

"Gain? It should be obvious. I will become the High Priest of Jubilee and thereby control the government of Jubilee, Pruvia and Mt. Mizaan just as you do. Finally, I will be victorious in having the power and status I fully deserve. You will not rule me, you will not have beaten me, and you will no longer reside on this island. After the battle, I will banish you and all the priests and their families to the mainland never to step foot on Jubilee again."

"I see. And I imagine that you have considered the fact that I did not select myself to be High Priest. In fact, as you well know, it is God and God alone who chooses the High Priest. What did you decide to do about that? How did you plan to handle God?"

"You always go there–you always bring God into the discussion. God will honor whoever is the High Priest and that my fond friend will be me."

"You never learn Natas. You never get the lesson. Everything is not about you. God reigns supreme on the earth and in the universe. You never fooled us Natas we were onto your scheme a long time ago we were just waiting, hoping and praying that you would come to your senses. Go onto the beach and look around. You will find that we are fully prepared to meet any onslaught that you conjure up. You need to know that your men on the west end have already been overcome as you will be in short order. In order to give you an opportunity to reconsider, I will meet you on the field at four o'clock as the sun begins to set."

"We'll be there Zar! We'll be there, and you can rest assured that I will come out the victor!"

Zar hung up the phone and turned to Bosher. "It's on brother. He's really full of himself this time. There's no getting out of it. Please alert Zadok, Batu, and Jezreel of his advance. We are to meet him for battle by four o'clock. Have all of them meet us in the Temple at three o'clock for prayer."

He left for the Temple immediately to dress and prepare for the battle that lay before them. He called his stable and gave direction to have Koach brought to Jubilee in preparation for the day at hand. He then prepared his priestly clothes as directed to wear during the battle. Truth be known, he really wanted to engage Natas in battle. He wanted the satisfaction of standing over him in clear defeat. He wanted him to say out loud, "You win!" He wanted to feel the power of his fists in his face, in throwing him down and around, of kicking him and hearing him wince, he wanted to feel the satisfaction of pummeling Natas' body time and time again. He stopped himself knowing that to consider such was not what God had planned and he had been warned to pray against the spirit of strife, vengeance, and anger that was trying to flourish; if it arose in him it would be his undoing. He knew that the battle was not his but The Lord's.

He began to recite: "I belong to the King of Kings. I am worthy of all good things because I serve the Lord willingly. I am the servant of God. I am the head and not the tail, and it is my will to have nothing to do with sin and evil. I serve the Master of the Universe. I am a priest of the Most High God. God's spirit flows in through and with me. My heart is clean, and I serve at the total pleasure of God Almighty. I am able to do all things through God's strength in my life. I am able to do as God directs in this battle. We will be victorious for God is with us; the banner of the Lord is our shield and our buckler. God is my strong tower." *Breathe. Breathe in the Word of God. This battle is the Lord's and is beyond your mortal understanding.*

Koach arrived and stood ready to be dressed for the encounter. He was an amazing animal; strong, sturdy and stable. Zar was proud to ride him into battle. He stood at attention as he was dressed with the garb of combat representing The Lord God Almighty; mighty in battle. He looked elegant, exquisite and well-bred donned with the array of God. Zar finished dressing and met the others in the Temple at three o'clock. They bowed out of respect for his office noticing the change to his official uniform as the High Priest. Bosher had also changed into his priestly garb and was ready to go before the Lord in prayer. In like manner, they followed Zar into the temple and bowed in reverent prayer. Zar prayed out loud, and they aligned their hearts, souls, and spirits with his.

"Father, we beseech you on this auspicious occasion to lead guide and direct our steps. Go before us Father and be our Strong Tower. We have the honor of representing you before the world. Lord, please fill us with your Spirit. Help us to represent you in all that we do and say in this hour. It is our will to be instruments in Your Hands for Your honor and Glory. Victory is ours in the name of the Lord. We reverence you, honor you, love, adore, serve and follow you, Father. In the words and thoughts of David, whom you loved so very much, we beseech you to keep our enemies from us; overcome them in your strength so that all will see the Glory of God. Amen." They each took a moment of solitude for themselves and then Zar, as the High Priest turned to them and blessed them. "The Lord bless and keep you; the Lord make His face to shine upon you and be gracious to you; the Lord turn His face upon you and give you peace."

They moved out to assemble with their troops on Pruvia. Natas moved his army into position at exactly four o'clock as the sun was setting. Zar mounted Koach, and from the east end of Pruvia together they strutted slowly onto the proposed battlefield. How glorious it all was! Koach dressed in gold and white sporting the emblems of God and Zar dressed in the full array of the priesthood sitting astride the most stalwart white stallion imaginable. It was breathtaking, and all that were there immediately knew that this was more than a battle between Zar and Natas for rulership of the Trinity Islands. No! This was a battle of profound proportions that went far beyond the two of them–this was a battle between truth and deception, darkness and light – God and Satan. The deceptions of Natas represented all the lies, sins and evil doings that Satan had fostered forever since the beginning of time. Natas had totally given himself over to the spirit of the evil one himself; he was fully consumed with negativity; selfishness and he had become most proficient at deception; a craft of the devil.

"So, you showed up as I expected you would. You are not one to turn down a good challenge; I was counting on that. As you can see you are outnumbered ten to one. Do you want to concede now or is it necessary for your men to lose their lives right here on the beach? Surely, you do not expect to win."

"Of course, I came to meet you son of perdition. It seems you will never surrender although you know full well that you have been overcome. I came not for you but to offer Grace and Mercy to any of those who stand with you prior to their demise. It is not the will of God that any should die."

"You've got to be kidding. You have the audacity to offer grace and forgiveness to those who are certain to win? You offer them a chance to live when it is a given that the battle is ours? Men! Stand ready for the assault at my direction. Spare no one but leave the horse and rider to me."

Zar could feel his men ready to move. They were well trained, and fear had no place in them. The fact that they were outnumbered did not faze them. He turned to them and held up his hand notifying them that they were not to advance. He spoke again to the army of Natas.

"If there is anyone among you who has not lost faith in Jehovah, who has knowledge of His Grace and Mercy and who is willing to acknowledge him by standing aside do so now. Our God is faithful and willing to extend himself to all who seek him with their whole heart. You men have been totally deceived by Natas, you have been caught in his web of lies, and the ultimate deception is that he has convinced you that somehow you will prevail against the will of God. Stand down and live! Think of the sin of it all; think of the actions you are prepared to take for one who knows no good thing;

the truth is not in him. Do you believe that he will live up to his promises? Surely, within you is a modicum of truth and honor. If, there is anyone who wishes to live and to come to know the true commander of all and His loving ways–stand aside and your lives will be spared."

"If anyone moves, I give the Captain of the army full permission to shoot him."

"Ah! There it is. There is the proof I speak of; he cares nothing for you. I promise that if you stand aside, if you come over you will be spared, and no harm will come to you. If you wish to come to honor Jehovah move out now; so that you will not be lost in the battle."

It was quiet until in the back of the line you heard a minor rustling, a bit of movement and a shout out, "I am on the Lord's side. I seek Grace and Mercy." Of the one thousand men gathered there only thirty of them stood aside. Only thirty sought God's forgiveness. As promised, nothing happened to them; they stood on the side near the soldiers of God. As they did, they were signaled to join them in the ranks for protection.

"Good. Let them go. I want everyone to notice that all will fall at my command even those who once were among us."

Zar turned to Zadok, Jezreel, and Batu, "Do not move until I say so. Do not spill one ounce of blood on this land as God has ordered. No blood of a human shall touch this land. He will overtake them by his own means." Hearing the command to charge from Natas, he turned to his men and lifted his hand to notify them not to move.

"Advance! Kill all of those who stand in our way. Spare no one!"

With that Natas' army took up arms and rushed toward those protecting Jubilee. As instructed the armies of God stood firm. On came the forces of evil; on came the satanic armies at full speed shouting all manner of invectives and chants. They did not notice the ominous cloud that had formed above them. They took no heed to the darkening of the sun or the shaking of the ground beneath them. On they ran with blood and hate filling their voices and their veins.

Seeing the advance of the army, Koach became agitated; he began to prance about striking the ground with his hooves. Incensed by the running forces, he reared on his hind feet striking the air as though in a fierce battle. Simultaneously, huge bolts of lightning flashed illuminating the scene below. Zar steadied himself and held onto the emboldened stallion. He kicked his feet and came down with a fierce thump, snorting, and whinnying and braying at the forces. When his hooves struck the earth, a loud rattling sound cracked through the earth opening a huge gorge which swallowed all the forces of Natas in one fell swoop. A vast cavern opened and scooped up the full army; just as quickly a massive wave gushed forth filling the great abyss and then receded. Seemingly, the huge wave rolled out to sea very calmly leaving a smooth beach front and no signs what-so-ever of the army of Natas.

When the encounter was over, the cloud rose and was replaced by brilliant rays that escaped to cover the earth. No one spoke. No one moved for what seemed like minutes. Finally, Zar raised the banner of God, patted Koach and turned to face the men of Jubilee.

"Our God is able to do all things! This is not the first time God has performed great miracles. Why do you stand in awe? Do not forget the great escape from Egypt at the Red Sea. Do not forget the parting of the Jordan River when natural men walked on dry land. Do not forget all of the numerous miracles our God has done for the sake of His people. Have you forgotten how the earth opened up and swallowed Korah and his men when they dishonored God? God is the reason for Jubilee. He is the reason that we have chosen to come aside from the mainland and live according to His Word."

"Men of Jubilee gather stones and build an altar here upon this land as a witness that God prevailed once again against the forces of evil. God will always protect those who are faithful to Him. It is why we choose to live in an environment that willfully honors the principles and tenets God has given us from the beginning. Honor God and be faithful to Him alone! All praise goes to God our strength in a time of trouble!"

Zar felt like the High Priest, and he was proud that he was able to overcome his internal struggle to engage in battle with Natas. *"Natas. To think he doesn't even exist anymore. It pays to be on The Lords' side."* He bent low and talked to Koach. "Good fella!'. You had an extraordinary day; quite memorable. I was very proud of you." Koach nodded his head as though he fully understood every word. He struck the earth with his right hoof and pranced off of the beach in his own magnanimous style with his owner sitting very erect. The men cheered and yelled out praises to God for their success, and then they disbanded into their separate units.

Each Captain, Jezreel, Batu, and Zadok addressed their men with pride as it pertained to their performances. They were told to report to base and then to assume their regular duties. They would all be given a full report in the next day or so.

Chapter Forty-Six

Zar could hardly wait to get home to Sierra and give her a full detailed report. Before he left for home and disrobed, he went into the Temple sanctuary, knelt down and spoke to God.

"Father thank you for allowing me to represent you today! Thank you for the success of the whole encounter. Oh! To be able to witness the power of our God; although it seems impossible, I have fallen more in love with you; more in awe of you. Breathe on me, Lord! Breathe your Spirit into me so that I might be able to lead your people forward. Today we encountered the full onslaught of Satan to take over and consume the Trinity Islands, but you would not allow it. Without your guidance, we would not have been able to withstand the battle. Father, please use me to strengthen your people as we grow. Bless me so that I might be able to bless your people. Thank you, Father, for allowing me to participate in the battle as You directed. I stand ready to do your will Your way. Amen."

After he changed his clothes, he hustled to get to Sierra. As he approached his father-in-law's home, she saw him and ran to meet him. "Hey! You shouldn't be running in your condition, should you?"

"Don't be silly Zar. I'm only six, maybe seven weeks pregnant. I'm fine. I missed you, and the whole village is buzzing. Come sit down and tell me everything."

"Okay. But please just take it easy. You're carrying my son." He smiled and held her close to him and then he sat down and tried as best he could to paint a careful picture of the whole event right down to the final dismantle of the troops. She was totally mesmerized; in absolute awe of the situation. "I'm so proud of you Zar and of the men of Jubilee. It is so clear that God loves us and that He will protect us from everything as long as we keep him first."

He entered the house and gave a full report to the family. They were all grateful for his safety and that God Almighty had reigned supreme on the islands. They knew he was exhausted and encouraged him to lie down and take a nap before dinner. Sierra went to prepare a bed for him and to hug and kiss him and tell him how very grateful she was that he was home and safe.

"Will Jubilee ever be the same again? She asked.

"In one way yes, it will. This community is closely knit together. I doubt that it will change. In another way, we will constantly be vigilant of our need to secure our lands and people. Instead of relaxing any standard as new people enter our portals, I will encourage everyone to strengthen our standards and to rehearse them. The principles on which we founded the Trinity islands are still prevalent and must be enforced to the nth degree. I love the diversity we have among us now, but we must not compromise our standards to incorporate others. If we do so, it will confuse the original families and lay question to the purpose of rules leaving them open to interpretation. Thus, sayeth The Lord; we must remain faithful. That must be our goal of demarcation."

She left the room and closed the door behind him knowing that he was tired. Silently she prayed and thanked God for bringing him back to her stronger and better than before.

###

In the meantime, Batu ran all the way home, and when he found her, he swept Ashima into his arms. *She is safe. Thank you, Lord. She is safe.* "I thought you were supposed to be with Deja? Is she here?" Ashima looked pleasantly surprised. "Why yes, she is. She's in the garden picking some fresh veggies for dinner." She stood on her toes and hugged her husband tightly.

"I'm so happy that you are home. You know you could have told me why you were so concerned. I know how to keep a secret." He looked down at her and scowled just a bit.

"Um Hmm. You and Deja are excellent at keeping secrets. Everything is over now, and we can all settle down. Things might change a bit but not much for the villagers. I'll keep you informed. Anything change around here? Are you okay?"

"Now that you are home, I'm fine. And I hope you noticed that the door was locked just as I promised I would do."

"I noticed, and I really thank you for keeping your word. You mean the whole world to me and I simply cannot have anything happen to you. Got anything to eat?"

"Go wash up, and I'll meet you at the table. We've been cooking since early morning in anticipation of your return."

###

Zadok never ran anywhere he didn't need to; he had long legs which took him wherever he wanted to go as quickly as he needed to get there. He was always prepared to run, and he could run quite fast but if there was no need, he simply didn't put his body through the rigors of running. He strolled up to Devine's house and knocked on the door. She opened the door, and her face lit up.

"Zadok! Zadok! You're home. We heard all about how God showed up at the battle and that not even one drop of blood was shed because just like He did when Korah and his men showed The Lord contempt, the earth opened up and swallowed them. Awesome! Praise God for His awesome strength and power. Praise God for him showing favor to Jubilee! Come inside."

He drew a deep breath and sat down next to her. It didn't take long for family and friends to find out that he was there and hustle themselves into the house for a full account of the day's events. Although he was tired, he knew that they were excited and filled with many questions. He took his time and told them as clearly as possible about the occurrence. After he completed his report, they all praised God shouting loudly, "Praise God from whom all blessings flow." Shortly thereafter, he whispered to Devine that he was going home to take a nap and would like to join them for dinner later if that was possible.

"Zadok! You're home now. A seat will always be reserved for you at the table. I can't wait to see you later after you're rested."

"I'll be there later filled with the anticipation of seeing you."

Kila spotted him first and then ran and alerted Seth and Libi that he was home. By the way he was walking she knew he was exhausted, but she still ran to him and jumped into his arms.

"Father, father, I am so happy that you are back and that you are safe." She squeezed his neck as hard as she could and kissed his cheeks several times. She welcomed him home like only little girls can with their fathers.

Libi was in the house, but she dropped everything and went to him. She didn't speak but simply opened her arms and hugged him ever so tightly for a long time. He responded in kind delighted to know that his family was safe and sound. It felt good to be home among the people he loved the most. The past several months had taken their toll on him; he was tired.

"Is Seth home?"

"Yes sir. I came as fast as I could." Seth seemed to have gotten taller since he was home the last time. His chest seemed to be a bit larger, and it looked like there were muscles developing in his young arms. He walked closer to Bosher and hugged him. "I'm so glad that you are home and safe. I tried to be vigilant and keep our home safe, but your shoes are too big for me yet."

"Seth, son it is really good to see you." He squeezed his arm which gave him a bit of resistance and said, "My, my! Seems there is a strong young man coming up in this house. My shoes won't be too big for you soon."

"My father has B-I-G shoes to fill. I don't fool myself that I'm anywhere near ready to even tie them. You look tired can I do something or get something for you?"

"Carry me to the bed son; carry me to the bed. But before that let's grab a bite to eat and I'll fill you all in on how things unfolded."

Kila and Libi had already gone into the kitchen to rustle up some food and were bringing plates to the table. They sat and ate and listened to the story of plans and battle strategies and the divisiveness of Natas and finally the reckoning of The Lord. He told them that he would take them to Pruvia in the next day or two so they could view the altar that was built in commemoration of the event. After they ate, they suggested that he lay down and that they would all meet up together later that evening. He agreed and eased up from the table and headed for the bedroom. Libi followed him and closed the door.

"That's a good wife. Come here and give me a proper welcome home."

"Yes sir! Right away sir!" She feigned a salute and entered his open arms. It felt good to be in his embrace, and she was ever so grateful that he was home and safe and available to them again. "You guys were all I could think of. I knew God would handle it, but in the natural, I was more than willing to lay it all on the line for my family if it came to it. My life has never been fuller and more complete than now, and I like it. Can you lay with me for a moment?"

"I thought you'd never ask. This house, this room is not complete without you. I've got to fix dinner and see to the kids, but I will lay here with you until you go to sleep. Which, I must say should not be too long from now." He nodded that she was probably right, pulled off his clothes and laid across the covers. As expected, she thought that he would be asleep in five…four…three…two…

Jezreel stopped by his house and freshened up before going to see Monave. He knew she would be at the shop. He went and retrieved Jet, and together they sauntered off toward the shop. He waited for just the right moment, and then he opened the door and let Jet into the shop. It didn't take long before Havi found that he was there and came out to play with him. Monave heard some noise and came out to find the two of them nuzzling each other over by the window.

"Hmm. Hi Jet! Where is your master?"

Jet looked up and then down and kept playing with Havi. "Jez, Jez! Where are you?" There was no response. "Okay, this is not the time for tricks. Come out here. I want to see you." No answer. He was not in the shop, so she went to the door looking for him. "Jezreel! Come out here." No answer. Frustrated she turned to go back into the shop and spotted him standing near the counter with his mouth full on little pie tarts.

"Um umm. Yum! I love these little pies. Hope I didn't wipe you out." He said with a big cheese-eating grin on his face.

"What? How'd you get in here? I looked everywhere for you?"

"Mystique! I'm a man of mystery. However, it is no mystery that I am head over heels in love with you, and I can't wait another moment for you to be my wife. That's some ring you're sporting young lady. The man who gave that to you must be totally infatuated with you."

"Jez. I'm so glad you're home I was really worried about you especially after I heard of the danger that you all just came through. No wonder you were going on recon all the time. I hope we never have to encounter anything like that again. I thank God that He loves us so much."

"I can't even begin to tell you the trials and tribulations we encountered. Maybe later, but now I just want to drink in the sight of you and to listen to you tell me when and where you want me to be for our marriage."

"We have it all figured out and I was just waiting for you to settle down and return so we could put everything into effect."

"I'm here now. Whatever you want is fine with me just make it soon. I'm lonely, and I need a wife. A good wife and you fit the bill perfectly."

She smiled and flashed her ring at him. "I hope you'll agree with me, but I want something a bit different than the norm. Something uniquely us."

"I'm game, what is it?"

She told him the plan, carefully painting a word picture that he could grasp. He liked it a lot and agreed. They planned to be married in three weeks.

"Yes! I finally win the prize. I'm delighted with your plans and will do everything you want to make it as special as you are. Got anything to eat? I'm starving."

"You just cleaned out my whole basket of pies. Come on and help me close up and we'll go home with our news and have dinner at the house. You know my mother; she'll have plenty of food and be happy that you're home to eat with us."

Chapter

Forty-Seven

Zar, the High Priest of Jubilee called a special congregational meeting for the next Sabbath at the Temple. All of the inhabitants of Jubilee joined together to praise and worship The Lord. Each of the divisional priests dressed in their full official garb and joined him in front of the altar of God. Uniformly they sang out praises to the only God who was worthy of all praises–Jehovah. Voices rang out in celebration of the day and in honor of God keeping His commitment to the forefathers of His people; Abraham, Isaac, Jacob from whom the twelve tribes emanated. Finally, Zar raised his hands to silence the people just before he spoke to them.

"People of God, children of Jubilee we have come through extremely difficult times for no other reason, but that God loves us. It is a great love that we as natural human beings who have known sin cannot fully appreciate or understand. All I know is that He cherishes those who chose to be obedient to His principles. We have committed to keeping those precious laws, standards, and rules that are the very foundation upon which we stand and govern Jubilee, and which shall always be our guiding principles. We have the written texts and Holy Scripts to guide us, and we have a strong history upon which to rely. Our forefathers chose this land to be unique and to give us an opportunity to worship God in Spirit and in Truth without interruption or personal interpretation. It is clear that God rules Jubilee. He resides with us and watches over the Trinity Islands. We are most blessed of the blessed among all of His people because just a few days ago He gave us yet another sign that He loves us and will protect us from all enemies who attempt to thwart His purpose for us.

As I reminded the armies who protect our borders, it is not the first time that God expressed His desire to keep us in perfect peace. The Old Testament continues to remind us of His Goodness and His Grace. Allow me a moment to recite from Psalm 78 as David wrote a brief history for us to be mindful of. David loved God and is reported to have been a man after God's own heart. Hear his words to us today. He begins by reminding us that our ancestors told us that we should record and retell the praiseworthy deeds of The Lord God Almighty throughout each generation.

Specifically, David tells us of the power of God, and of the many wonders, God has done for His people. When needed to sustain His people, God decreed statutes for Jacob and laws to rule Israel which God commanded our ancestors to teach their children, generation following generations: it is so even to this day in Jubilee. The reason He commanded this recital was so that the people of God would put their trust in Him and keep His commandments. David reminds us that the men of Ephraim did not keep God's covenant and did not keep His laws because they did not rehearse the laws or commandments as they were told so that they eventually forgot what God had done for them and the wonders God had shown to them. They forgot that God alone divided the Red Sea and led them through on dry land making the water to stand up on either side like a wall. They forgot that God was a cloud by day and fire at night to keep them protected from the elements. Yes! They even forgot that God split the rocks in the wilderness and gave them water to drink; He brought streams of water out of the rock. In spite of all these miracles as they walked through the desert, the people complained to Him about their wants and needs. Can you believe it? These stiff-necked ancestors of ours continued to rebel against our God. "We want bread," so, God created manna the "Food of Heaven" for them. "We want meat" so he gave them fowl and still they rebelled against His goodness. When God turned His anger on them because of their consistent sinning they would ask for forgiveness and flatter Him with their mouths while lying with their tongues; their hearts were not loyal to Him, they were not faithful to His covenant. Time and again, God restrained his anger against them because he remembered that they were but flesh. God tumbled Egypt to almost total ruin in order to bring his people out into the land of promise driving out nations so he could allot them land as an inheritance. Did they keep His statutes and commandments? No! They still had rebellion in their hearts, but God, full of Grace and Forgiveness continued to love them. Through fires, flood, wars, and tumult of every sort and type until God found David who loved God and led the people with integrity of heart.

The story is not over; we know it well even up until this very day. We fully understand why we chose to leave the mainland and to live according to God's commandments and statutes with His people. Today we stand free to worship Him openly and fully. Yesterday, evil rose its ugly head and tried to overcome us for no good purpose and as in times of old God advanced against it to the full protection of us–the people of God here on Jubilee. We must never forget the lessons of old; they are still pertinent and relevant for us today, perhaps even more so. Stand firm on our purpose. Stand firm for our rules and statutes which were given to us by God. Stand firmly committed to honoring Him with all of your heart begging Him day–by–day to give you a clean heart so that you might worship Him. People of Jubilee praise and worship God with all of your being – He is worthy!"

When Zar completed his message, the people shouted with joy to the God of Heaven and earth who they loved and served. Zar and all the priesthood turned from them and bowed in total praise and worship to the god that they loved and adored uttering words of praise and honor to their Maker, Lord, and King.

Chapter
Forty-Eight

When morning arrived, after he had rested through the night, he kissed Sierra and told her that he must get to Mount Mizaan. He told her that he was uncertain exactly how many days he would be gone but would hurry back as quickly as possible. He asked her to stay with her parents, but she refused and reported that she wanted to go to their vacation home on Mount Mizaan and that she would wait for him there. He agreed.

He was in a rush to get to the top of the mountain to speak with God but knew he had to wait until he was summoned. One didn't rush in on God and say, "Excuse me, but I need to speak to you." First off as you approached the top of the mountain, you were most surely on holy ground. Secondly, he was not certain if you could disturb God, but he did know he wasn't going to be the one to find out. These were unusual circumstances which did not include simple prayer in talking to God; it was much more than that. When you were on the crest of the mountain it was most definitely by invitation–God "Called you" because He had a reason or a specific mission for you to handle. So... he breathed deeply and calmed down. He glanced around and took in the awesome beauty of the mountain and waited to speak with his Father. It did not take long.

"Come up Jezreel I'm waiting for you. Meet with me on the top of the mountain tomorrow at the break of dawn."

His soul rejoiced as he speedily positioned himself as close to the top of the mountain as possible so that when he awoke in the morning, he would be certain to be on time for his meeting. He laid down in the plush green carpet of grass that was beneath him. It smelled delightful and felt like a bounty of green goodness. As he lay there, he could not help but notice how clear the skies were not at all like the day of the Great Advance against Jubilee. Soft, white, puffy, opulent clouds floated here and there. He thought awhile and recalled how the Book of Nahum referred to clouds as, "The dust from God's footprints." The air did not seem like air at all; although the air on Jubilee was quite pristine, clean and clear. Clouds, beautiful shapely clouds were in abundance. Clouds were a constant reminder that God was everywhere.

He remembered that God always came in a cloud; He never came in the clear shining of the day–but rather always in a cloud. He closed his eyes and thought about God in deep and moving ways. He had learned a lot from the lesson with Natas. Specifically, that his relationship with God must be right and that his external expression of his relationship with God must also be right. *"Challenging,"* he thought but essential. He had learned to conquer his emotions and think when faced with spiritual obstacles. When negative thoughts clouded his mind and flamed his emotions, he had learned to be still and revisit what God had taught him. He had discovered that when he could quiet himself and think about to whom he was praying, he was able to advance spiritually.

He cherished the time he spent on the mountain. The air on Mount Mizaan was filled with the scents of different types of sweet perfumes; it reminded him of what the incense in the Temple must have smelled like when Aaron and other priests burnt the offering which represented the prayers of the people of God. He knew that the incense in the Temple was special and holy unto God. He knew the scented compounds well. Holy Incense was made of equal parts of; stacte, onycha, galbanum, and frankincense. The air on Mount Mizaan smelled familiar like that yet; there was an added ingredient he could not determine.

Mount Mizaan's air was light, fresh and new. New like a brand-new baby; fresh and clean. New like the day after a fresh, invigorating rain had fallen and kissed the earth with promise all whipped up with the smell of Holy Incense. It was relaxing and absolutely wonderful.

He settled down and thought about the events of the Great Advance. He pondered what made men so evil; what made Natas choose to live a life that was an affront to God especially when he had so much going for him. He was wealthy, handsome, multi-talented exceeding in almost everything he set out to do; but nothing seemed to satisfy him. Why? He simply could not imagine why it was not enough. What was it in a man's heart and soul that made him envy and covet, lie and steal from others? Why were God's laws so difficult for some to consider when there were many others who dedicated their lives to Him? Life could be so beautiful when you submitted to the will of God for your life. He had spent many days and nights trying to figure it out to no avail.

He was ecstatic about being born during a time when his forefathers had the wisdom to pull away from the mainland so that their families could try to live according to the laws of God. He was totally committed to leading the people on the Trinity Islands in the ways of Jehovah. However, when he reviewed the activities associated with the Great Advance against Jubilee, he knew that they had to guard their lives more stringently because of the nature of man. He knew that there would be other threats to the islands simply because they were beautiful and wealthy, clean, clear, bursting with opportunity to flourish. He wanted to talk to God about it and take his lead from Him. The night began to encroach upon the daylight as he nestled into the soft billowy green grass. It did not take long for him to fall asleep once he began dreaming of Sierra and his new baby boy.

Just as the sun peaked its head over the brink of the earth waking the floret of flowers and fauna, he opened his eyes to a fresh new day. He freshened up quickly and took off galloping up the path to the crest of the mountain. He arrived at the platform and waited. It was not long before that special cloud that housed the Spirit of God appeared.

"Good morning son. I am happy that you slept well and are refreshed after such a tumultuous time on Jubilee. I know you have many questions and I am here for you."

Zar could never get used to the fact that he had an audience with the God of the whole universe. "Father thank you so very much for taking the time to speak with me. I hope that I was able to fulfill your plans as you laid them out. Just as you warned me, I had to overcome my own desires to engage in battle with Natas. I prayed ardently, and you helped me to calm down and let you have your way in the matter."

"Zar, you are a good and faithful son as I knew you would be well before you were formed in the belly of your mother. I had need of you for such a time as this. Every trial, every test was laid before you in order to build your spiritual muscles and your faith in me. You have not failed me; you have done well, and I am well pleased. However, just as you suspected there will be others that will see the peace and promise in the Trinity Islands and especially Jubilee. There will be other attempts to seize them from you. This is my pledge to you; as long as you follow my rules, laws, and statutes, no one will ever be able to snatch

you or those on the islands from me. I am your God; your Father; there is none like me. I am the great I AM. I love you! I love who you are and how you are and what is more, even in your imperfection–much like David–I know that you love me. Pray often and stay tuned into Me for when I need you again, I shall call you to come up."

"Thank you. Thank you for being my father and my friend. Thank you for Sierra and the baby and for the life I have with family and friends. Please order my steps so that I will not fail you or them. Please help me to have a clean heart so that I may worship you with truth and honesty."

"You are never alone. I have many on Jubilee and on the mainland, who love me as you do, and I have a mission for each of them. Go now; you, my son are blessed among all men as I have chosen you to serve me in spirit and in truth as you have requested."

With that the foreground of the cloud shone a brilliant, dazzling sun drenching light and when he blinked it was gone. He stood there on the crest of the mountain with his shoes off to the side; hands at his side, his head bent up towards heaven and his mouth open whispering praise and thanksgivings to the only wise God there was. Reverently he bowed as he backed down the mountain crest and steadied himself. He didn't know why God loved him; didn't know why God cared about him but he was eternally grateful that He did. He looked all about, took everything in and then decided to leave for home immediately.

Chapter Forty-Nine

Just as he expected he found Sierra on the beach astride Allure. The two of them made such a beautiful picture with the ocean, sky, and mountains as their backdrop. He hustled down to the stable and retrieved Koach who was obviously delighted to see him. He saddled up, and the two of them sauntered down the beach until they met with them. Sierra was obviously quite pleased that her husband had returned to her and Allure pranced in place as Koach came up beside her. Sierra did not speak immediately but simply leaned close to him and kissed him gently.

"I'm so happy that you are home. I'm never quite complete when you are away from me. By the looks of you all went well. You're simply glowing."

"Yes, it did go well. I am always so amazed that I could actually be speaking with God. I'll tell you all about it later. How are you feeling?"

"Wonderful! Warm and lovely, happily married to the man of my dreams and as always I'm hungry."

He reached out and touched her stomach. "We can fix that. How'd you like me to fix you the best meal of a lifetime?"

"Do you know how to cook?"

"My dear, this is no time for foolishness. Of course, I know how to cook. You are in for a treat. Come on. Let me get you settled down and prepped for a sumptuous meal."

They left for the house and a quiet and loving evening together. Later after the meal which she raved about, she told him that Zadok and Devine had announced that they were getting married. The wedding was to be quiet and special just for intimate family and friends. They were eager to go and spent much of the evening discussing what they thought would be an appropriate wedding gift for two such unique individuals.

A few weeks past and the day of the wedding approached quickly. Both Zadok and Devine wanted something intimate and special. They wanted some quiet time with family and friends to remember for the future. Zadok was relatively conservative and decided that whatever she wanted would suffice as long as they got married quickly. They found a wonderful facility on the east end of the island that had just recently been built. They incorporated all of the ceremonial portions of the wedding under the Chuppah with Zar as the priest in charge and Bosher rendering the special blessing. They loved both of them dearly.

Rather than invite the whole community to engage in the celebration, they trimmed the guest list down to about two hundred and fifty intimate family and friends which obviously included Zadok's whole troop, temple elders and their families, family from the mainland for each of them, etc. They fully enjoyed themselves. Devine was spectacular which was not hard for her to do since she was so captivatingly beautiful. Her headdress was consumed of her favorite color of shades of purples draped over a soft white gown that flowed with every step she made.

Zadok dressed in his military white officers' uniform making a striking figure of a man; especially her man. They melted together as they walked away to begin their life together as man and wife. They wouldn't tell anyone where they were going afraid that somehow her family would show up at the site. You could hear them laughing as they walked away. She fit neatly beneath his arm which was wrapped around her waist so she could be close to him. They left the laughter, the food, and dance and the frivolous gestures associated with a wedding and stepped into a new beginning as man and wife. Zadok and Devine-finally together as planned from the beginning.

Exactly four weeks from the wedding of Zadok and Devine Jezreel and Monave prepared for their wedding. For Jubilee, it would definitely be a bit different but different could be a good thing–and it was for this memorable occasion. The Chuppah was made of a special type of fabric that looked like glass; it sparkled and sent off brilliant shards of light whenever the sun struck it. It was situated on a specially built platform on the beach front of Jubilee. All around the Chuppah were stations for chairs and artifacts that accompanied the design of the wedding décor. Plants were staged all around the Chuppah and at purposeful sites between chairs and aisles. It was stupendous! Spectacular! It was simple elegance all wrapped in one holy event. A trail of white fabric carpeted the platform leading from the pier to the main event under the Chuppah.

The celebration began in grand fashion. All the guests were quite impressed and felt like the surrounding environment was the perfect fit for the couple. It was different and favorably accepted. As expected, Cherish was the Maid of Honor for her sister. Ardash stood in the office of her father with tears clearly threatening to explode at any moment. Jaya stood by dressed in a dazzling soft pink outfit praying silently for her daughter to be blessed and happy. Jezreel's family had turned out in numbers to enjoy and celebrate the marriage of one so well loved. Her brothers stood by in silence for once; no joking was noticed. And Mingo, the town entertainer, was somber remembering Monave as they grew up–memories flooded his mind, and he was delighted for his youthful school mate.

The couple took their places under the Chuppah. They all agreed that Zar would officiate over the wedding and that Bosher would give the final blessing. Monave looked statuesque dressed in a design of her own making. The fabric was from a foreign port which was white with threads of opal and silver punctuating the creases and crevices of the gown every now and again. Her head shawl was of the same fabric with huge white orchids gently pulling back the corners near her brow. Underneath the shawl was a thin plain white satin and silk band that spread from side to side of her forehead magnifying her huge doe-like eyes; she was beautiful by every stretch of the imagination. At the end of the celebration, cages of white doves which were hung above the corners of each of the four poles of the Chuppah were released into the wild celebrating the freeing of their souls to finally be together in wedded bliss.

Food and soft music were in abundance. Family and friends fully enjoyed the open and airy beachfront environment. It was a bit quieter than the normal wedding celebration; a bit more serene in its tempo and flow for a wedding celebration on Jubilee which made it symbolic of Monave's style and Jezreel's cool and easy manner. Free and easy that was them. Jezreel and Monave–clean and clear, open and honest in their dealings with each other and their friends. The wedding emulated the way they were. He was totally enamored with her, and she had waited patiently, feeding and stuffing his face, until he finally came to his senses and knew he wanted her for his wife.

Before they left for their honeymoon, they panned the area and spotted them on the pier together. Jet sat at attention looking on while Havi sat between his legs with his right paw on top of Jet's as usual. They looked at each other as they strolled toward the pier and knew–for certain–that once again all was right with their world.

Chapter

Fifty

Zar rose early in the morning and eased out of bed. Next to him, Sierra laid sleeping soundly after having nursed their newborn son. She cuddled the baby beneath her arm as he nestled against his mother listening to the familiar beat of her heart. He smiled and lingered for a while drinking in the sight of the two most important people in his earthly life. He adored them and silently whispered, *"Thank You!"* to his Father. He had rested well but was unable to get into a deep, sound sleep. He decided to dress, go down to the barn and take Koach for a ride. He scribbled a note to Sierra letting her know that he was fine and should return soon. He folded it neatly and left it on the pillow.

He arrived at the barn a bit before dawn. He patted Allure, gave her an apple and some fresh water and then went to retrieve Koach. Koach waited patiently, never losing sight of every step his master took. He bobbed his head a few times shaking his frothy mane about in preparation for a ride.

Zar approached him taking in the whole expanse of the huge animal. He was used to the animal, had ridden him many times, understood his temperament and yet this morning, he had a new, respect for the animal, the tool that God had used to end the siege against Jubilee. He became keenly aware that everything that breathed had the spirit of God within. Living plants and creatures could live and die, and thus, some portion of the Source of Life existed within them. He had always known that but when he gazed on Koach this time, he had a new perspective of him – a heightened awareness of the Spirit of God that lived within him. He reached out and touched his head, rubbed him gently, stroked his ears and spoke softly to him.

"I thank God for the opportunity to have been a part of this experience with you. You were exceptional and magnificent. I am eternally grateful for your commitment and devotion to me. What an honor to ride the beast that God selected to effectuate the final reckoning."

He guided Koach to the barn opening and into the newly awakening day. Together they rode off toward the beach to welcome the brilliance of another day. They were not disappointed-the day was glorious. No sooner than the cock had crowed the sun framed the day in glory. He rode the length of the shore pacing along effortlessly. Eventually, they came to a huge boulder. Zar dismounted Koach and moved to sit on the boulder for a quiet moment or two.

"Reflections. Memories. Remembering experiences are vitally important", he mused. The past few months had been arduous on so many fronts. He wondered, *"What makes a man so bent on doing evil? Natas had absolutely everything; money, exceptionally good looks, brilliant mental acumen, skilled in every sport imageable and yet none of it satisfied him. He knew spiritual principle better than most. Had opportunities that most would kill for and nothing was enough. Why did negativity and abasement hide in the souls of men?"*

His whole purpose was to please God and yet; there was always this diabolic predisposition hanging in the balance. He paused for a moment remembering the anger he felt toward Natas and the overwhelming desire to strike him, hurt and harm him although he knew those feelings were not the responses that God would have him consider. It took all of his personal restraint and mounds of prayer to get himself under control. He would never understand the nuances of sin. However, he knew that without any explanation at all, that sin existed now- as it always had. The only recourse, the only viable answer was to have a very personal relationship with God. Only He could thwart the Tempters Snares.

"How will I ever be able to lead the people of Jubilee? Who am I to carry such an overwhelming responsibility? I am only one man…one man who prays to be able to please God." He wanted to be able to hear his Father say, **"Well done my good and faithful servant; enter into the joy of the Lord."** Thoughts about the trials and tribulations of the past few months sieged his heart, and he felt faint to go on. He sank to his knees and just breathed in and out for minutes doing nothing; just being still.

Slowly, ever so slowly he began to smell the air, hear the waves and the call of nature about him. He looked down and viewed a tiny little ant bustling back and forth taking a weeny little piece of some substance into a hole in the boulder. He was working feverishly - back and forth, back and forth focused on one specific task. Quietly, Zar became aware of the awesomeness of God in his surroundings. He thought, *"What a tremendous treasure we have in Nature. In every wind that blows, in every night and day of the year, in every sunrise and rainbow, in every blossoming and withering of the earth- God comes to us. A flower, a tree or a little ant can convey a message of God."* He recalled that Songbirds were taught to sing in the dark. He considered whether we are often put into the shadow of God's hand until we learn to distinguish his voice. He decided that darkness was a time to listen. He was grateful for the times that God had blessed him and called him to "Come Up." There, on Mount

Mizaan he listened to the Voice of God and did as he was instructed. He realized that the Trinity Islands had not been saved because of anything that he had done. No! God had used him to fulfill a specific purpose just as he had used Koach and the armies of Jubilee throughout the whole ordeal.

Zar stood to his feet, took a deep breath and totally realized that he had never carried the full weight of Jubilee. He had never been alone. It was not up to him to "save" the islands from the villains of the future. Jubilee belonged to God. The people who resided on the Trinity Islands belonged to God - he was just an instrument in His Hands. Grateful for the opportunity to serve Him, he raised his hands, closed his eyes and prayed a silent prayer of gratitude for the whole experience.

As he mounted Koach, the huge white stallion pranced in place. He patted him several times and confidently said, "God always wins – always." With that, he headed for home where the tender warmth of a loving wife and a small bundle of baby blessing awaited him. He knew in his heart that God was always available to him and that he was never alone. As long as God had wanted him to, he would serve as the High Priest of Jubilee – God's vacation home.

Acknowledgements

My publisher, Debra Funderburk at Burkwood Media Group, truly lives up to her reputation to coach others to write and to make their books their business. She is a patient, loving, guiding spirit who has the blessed gift of leadership without judgment. She allows people to "express themselves" and finds a way to make it happen for them.

I asked Pastor Godwin Mitchell and his wife Gasie Mitchell to review the book, for the spiritual message and render an honest and open opinion. One day when we were exiting the church, he said, "You can write! Yes! You're an author." I was a bit surprised, but it encouraged me in ways he will never know. I respect his intellect and spiritual foothold on biblical principle. When I needed it, God sent a word via Godwin Mitchell. Thank You!

Thank you to The Charlotte Writing Academy, Charlotte Writer's Club, Christian Writers Institute, and many writer Meet-Up groups in the Charlotte area.

About the Author

Janet Perkins is an author, CEO of a Non-profit, wife, mother of five, grandmother of six, entrepreneur and inspirational leader. Her passion has always been writing to encourage others "To Look up from whence cometh their help." She is an avid reader and known as a "professional student."

Her first published book <u>- Through the Fire and the Flood: Marriage in the Midst of the Storm</u> has been widely received as a profile that encourages married couples to wade through "the challenges" and cling to each other. She has a purple passion for helping others and lends her many talents to those in need of assistance.

Janet writes only when given a "message" from The Master and is thrilled to be used as an instrument to encourage others in their spiritual walk. She has learned what it means to write under the unction of the Holy Spirit and prays to continue to be used to the glory of God.

She lives in Matthews, NC with her husband C.W. and new puppy Java.

www.ingramcontent.com/pod-product-compliance
Lightning Source LLC
Chambersburg PA
CBHW071347290426
44108CB00014B/1463